Loudenne

LA BOUCHERIE

THE KITCHEN

THE GREEN DINING ROOM

THE BIG HARVEST ROOM

FRENCH
COUNTRY COOKING

FRENCH COUNTRY COOKING

MEALS AND MOMENTS *from* A VILLAGE IN THE VINEYARDS

MIMI THORISSON

PHOTOGRAPHS BY ODDUR THORISSON

CLARKSON POTTER / PUBLISHERS

Also by Mimi Thorisson

A KITCHEN IN FRANCE

Published in the United States by Clarkson Potter / Publishers,
an imprint of the Crown Publishing Group, a division of
Penguin Random House LLC, New York.
crownpublishing.com
clarksonpotter.com

CLARKSON POTTER is a trademark and POTTER with colophon is a registered
trademark of Penguin Random House LLC.

Library of Congress Cataloging-in-Publication Data
Names: Thorisson, Mimi, author. | Thorisson, Oddur, photographer.
Title: French country cooking: meals and moments from a village in the
   vineyards / Mimi Thorisson; photographs by Oddur Thorisson.
Description: First edition. | New York : Clarkson Potter / Publishers, [2016]
   | ©2016 | Includes index. | Includes bibliographical references and index.
Identifiers: LCCN 2016004585 | ISBN 9780553459586 (hardcover) | ISBN
   9780553459593 (ebook)
Subjects: LCSH: Cooking, French. | Cooking—France—Mâedoc. | Thorisson,
   Mimi—Homes and haunts—France—Médoc. | Wineries—France. | LCGFT:
   Cookbooks.
Classification: LCC TX719 .T47285 2016 | DDC 641.5944—dc23 LC record
available at http://lccn.loc.gov/2016004585

ISBN 978-0-553-45958-6
eBook ISBN 978-0-553-45959-3

Printed in China

Book design by Jennifer K. Beal Davis
Photograph on page 17 by Ari Magg
Cover design by Jennifer K. Beal Davis and Stephanie Huntwork
Cover photographs by Oddur Thorisson
Illustrations by Amélie Claire

10 9 8 7 6 5 4 3 2 1

First Edition

FOR MY FAMILY

BÂTIR SALON AVANT CUISINE
DE LA MAISON C'EST LA RUINE.

TO BUILD THE LIVING ROOM BEFORE THE KITCHEN
OF THE HOUSE WOULD BE RUIN.

—PROVERB COLLECTED BY THE COUNT OF NEUFCHÂTEAU

CONTENTS

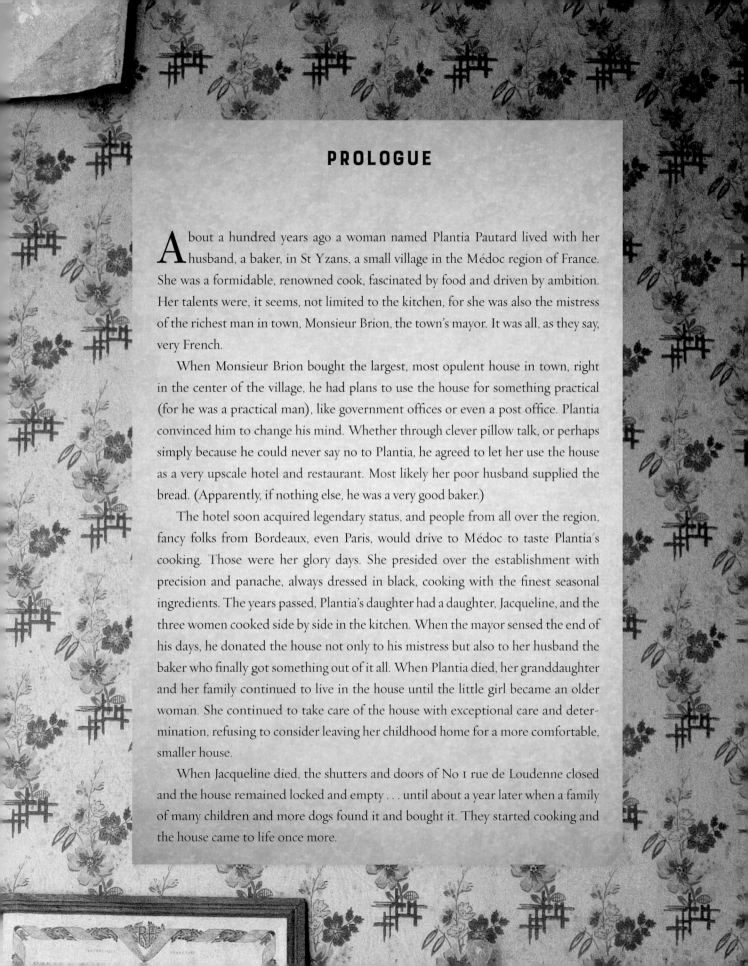

PROLOGUE

About a hundred years ago a woman named Plantia Pautard lived with her husband, a baker, in St Yzans, a small village in the Médoc region of France. She was a formidable, renowned cook, fascinated by food and driven by ambition. Her talents were, it seems, not limited to the kitchen, for she was also the mistress of the richest man in town, Monsieur Brion, the town's mayor. It was all, as they say, very French.

When Monsieur Brion bought the largest, most opulent house in town, right in the center of the village, he had plans to use the house for something practical (for he was a practical man), like government offices or even a post office. Plantia convinced him to change his mind. Whether through clever pillow talk, or perhaps simply because he could never say no to Plantia, he agreed to let her use the house as a very upscale hotel and restaurant. Most likely her poor husband supplied the bread. (Apparently, if nothing else, he was a very good baker.)

The hotel soon acquired legendary status, and people from all over the region, fancy folks from Bordeaux, even Paris, would drive to Médoc to taste Plantia´s cooking. Those were her glory days. She presided over the establishment with precision and panache, always dressed in black, cooking with the finest seasonal ingredients. The years passed, Plantia's daughter had a daughter, Jacqueline, and the three women cooked side by side in the kitchen. When the mayor sensed the end of his days, he donated the house not only to his mistress but also to her husband the baker who finally got something out of it all. When Plantia died, her granddaughter and her family continued to live in the house until the little girl became an older woman. She continued to take care of the house with exceptional care and determination, refusing to consider leaving her childhood home for a more comfortable, smaller house.

When Jacqueline died, the shutters and doors of No 1 rue de Loudenne closed and the house remained locked and empty . . . until about a year later when a family of many children and more dogs found it and bought it. They started cooking and the house came to life once more.

❧ NO 1 RUE DE LOUDENNE ❧

I had passed the gray, grand old house at No 1 rue de Loudenne on several occasions since moving to Médoc, but I had never thought that it would ever have anything to do with me.

We had left our Parisian lives a few years earlier and had settled in a farmhouse in the northern part of Médoc, right in the middle of the dense pine forests and close to the beautiful white beaches of the Atlantic coast. We had entered a mysterious new world of winemakers, hunters, vegetable growers, and local gourmands whose way of life seemed in many ways more content, simpler, and perhaps fuller than we had any right to expect. We were, in a word, happy! Our growing family felt at home in the countryside, and as the years passed we realized that we would probably never leave. We thought about buying a farmhouse to call our own, maybe something closer to the vineyards we love. It had to be special; it had to suit us.

Our friend Fabien, a local winemaker with a huge appetite and appreciation for life and all it has to offer, took matters into his own hands. He said, "You should live closer to us," probably because he had one eye on popping in for lunch now and then when he'd tire of working the tractor in his vineyards. A few days later, on a sunny, warm, late-January Monday, Oddur and I were driving around with Fabien's childhood friend, Stéphane, a local real estate agent who knows the twisted back roads of Médoc as well as anyone. He had three properties shortlisted for us. While they were all pretty enough, none was love at first sight, and it had to be. He was a little disappointed, and we seemed, I imagine, difficult to please.

On the way back home the car was silent. I realized that though I hadn't really gotten my hopes up, now that nothing had appealed to me, I felt a little let down; I had been so sure we'd easily find something we'd like. Halfway back home, Stéphane started saying something, then stopped. Moments later he hesitantly continued, "There is one house that is absolutely not what you are looking for, but something tells me you might like it. I don't have the keys, but do you mind if we go back and take a quick look?" He told us the house was in the village of St Yzans. Since we have always liked that part of Médoc, the wine country close to St Estèphe, we felt we had nothing to lose.

Ten minutes later we entered through the rusty, rambling gates of No 1 rue de Loudenne and found ourselves amongst the weeds and poorly maintained rose-bushes that lined the walls of the house. Stéphane explained to us that the building was empty and gave us a brief version of the history of it. Originally a winemaking château, it was once a hotel and restaurant and finally a family home. He told us that it had been lived in for years by a tough old lady who had died the year before, and now the estate was in the hands of her only son. He offered to call the owner who lived nearby if we wanted to look inside. Oddur hesitated; it just seemed like too much house, too farfetched (and he never thinks *anything* is farfetched)—we had been looking for a farmhouse, not a former château in the middle of a quiet village—but I just *needed* to see this house.

As we waited patiently in the garden, an elderly man, walking so slowly that he didn't really seem to be moving, advanced alongside the house up the street that leads to the cemetery. He stopped right in front of the gate, adjusted his sailor's cap, and stared at me for about a minute. He didn't gesture for me to come closer; he didn't seem to want to enter. He just seemed to be assessing the situation. Our eyes met and he gave me the faintest smile, as if to say, "I'm the past of St Yzans, and if you want to be the future, you have my blessing." Then he turned without saying a word and continued his stroll.

Monsieur Ladra, the very pleasant, slightly plump, and always well-dressed owner of the house, arrived minutes later with a big smile on his kind, teddy bear face. Within minutes he had disclosed his family's whole history, the account of how, through his great-grandmother's dalliance, the house had become family property. Then he gave us the grand tour. The big, faded, blue-green door that opens up into the central staircase seemed stuck, perhaps a last attempt by this old dame of a build-ing to keep her independence. But she relented and, once inside, as I gazed up the staircase, I knew I would live here, forever. The tiles beneath my feet were so pretty, the staircase right out of a fairy tale with faded, peeling wallpaper, and a bright blue light piercing through the window shutters on the second-floor landing. The house seemed much bigger from inside than it had from the courtyard, the corridors so wide, the ceilings so high. Stéphane led us up a dodgy ladder to the terrace on the roof—which he called "*la cerise sur le gâteau,*" the cherry on the cake—with wonderful views of the vineyards and even, on a clear day, of the Gironde estuary.

But for me, what sealed the deal was the kitchen. So much history buried in the cupboards and in the old tiles peeking out from under a modern linoleum flooring. A fireplace so large and inviting. What food I could make here! Where Stéphane saw great value and renovating possibilities, where Oddur saw beauty and flawless light, I saw nothing but steaks and duck breasts grilling in the fireplace; pots simmering on a stove; baskets filled with onions, parsnips, and potatoes; garlic and hams hanging from the ceilings. I saw myself cooking feasts in that kitchen.

Monsieur Ladra spoke lovingly of his mother, grandmother, and great-grandmother, Plantia, all of whom had been passionate, accomplished cooks. Plantia had run a hotel and restaurant and, according to him, the food had been legendary. He took us to the part of the house where the guest rooms had been, the numbers still on the doors, each one equipped with a porcelain sink. Some of the furniture was even still there, in all its termite-eaten glory. He enjoyed telling us tales of big shots from Bordeaux who used to come up north for the hunting season, unaccompanied by their wives. These gentlemen spent their mornings hunting, their lunches feasting on Plantia's food, and the evenings enjoying the fine wines of the region and, of course, the company of the ladies. He told us the house had been occupied by the Germans in the war, that at one time they'd had palm trees in the garden and a big sign on the side of the house that said "Hôtel de France." By the end of our tour, Monsieur Ladra told us we could keep any furniture we liked and offered to lend us a key so we could take a look whenever we wanted. As one last sales pitch, he casually added, "I have many of the old photographs from the good old days, and maybe I can even find some of my great-grandmother's recipes." The last bit caught my attention.

That night there was no discussion of "Should we?" Our fate was already sealed.

Very soon after we offered on the property, Monsieur Ladra, true to his word, gave us the keys. He added, "You're not really supposed to, but if you want to start work on it, just go ahead. This house is yours now; do with it what you want." It became a favorite pastime to visit the house, drive through the vineyards that lead to St Yzans, imagine what if would feel like to drive that road when we'd actually be on our way home. Many Sunday afternoons were spent having "picnics" in the "Salle des Vendanges"—the harvest room, where years ago the women of the Ladra

family cooked for sweaty and hungry harvesters. Next to the harvest rooms they had showers for the workers, and we decided early on that we'd keep at least one booth intact. It has a nice ring to it: lunch and a shower.

On one visit we discovered that although the house was technically not inhabited didn't mean it was completely deserted. A bat had taken up lodgings in a small, windowless room on the second floor that seemed to be an in-house antiques shop, filled with all sorts of curiosities: a French flag, old syringes, a crib, and numerous dressers. None of us is enchanted by bats, including the dogs who can't really catch them (though not for lack of trying), and just knowing about that creature put us in a state of constant alert. Our son, Hudson, more scared than any of his five sisters, ran screaming through the corridors of the house on many occasions—to the great pleasure of his competitive younger sister Louise.

While the bat ruled inside, a black cat had taken to guarding the front door. She was always there when we arrived, and when she saw us she would slip elegantly into the basement, through the slightly open shutters that lead to the wine cellar. I started calling her Plantia, imagining that the former mistress of the house was checking in on the new owners.

Sometime in late summer the bat was gone, and though the rest of the family was relieved, I realized I missed her; somehow she added a touch of derelict glamour that only bats and ghosts can provide. At least Plantia had taken up residence in our vegetable garden and didn't seem to be going anywhere.

ST YZANS is a small, quiet village, so quiet that people who visit us often ask if anyone else lives here. During my visits that first summer, I occasionally ran in to a villager or two. They were usually as curious as I was; they had heard we were coming and they wanted to know more. It was that mix of anticipation and caution. "It's our village, but you are welcome," they could have said.

One early summer's day I finally encountered the old man from that first time we had toured the house. His name was Monsieur Gilet, and he had lived all his life in the village. Madame Ladra, the one who had just passed away, had been his teacher at school, and later he had installed all the electricity in the house. He spoke fondly of the food that he had enjoyed there, especially the fava bean soup. "Everybody knew that Madame Pautard was an excellent cook," he said, talking about Plantia and her daughter. Mostly he spoke about his deceased wife, who was now resting in the cemetery down the road where he went twice every day despite his walking difficulties and where he spent a good deal of time before slowly heading back.

A friend introduced me to the town's mayor, Monsieur Segundo Cimbrone, one of the last communists in the region, who welcomed me with open arms. His wife, Conchita, had worked in the vineyards when she was younger, only, she said, "to be able to attend the harvest lunches at 1 rue de Loudenne." Little by little, week by week, I slowly met everybody, and most of them had something to say about our future home. Mr. Souslikoff, the mustachioed mechanic who loves old Citroëns, remembered how 1 rue de Loudenne was the only house with a telephone and how he'd been allowed to go there on two occasions with his parents to place important calls. Monsieur Teyssier, who owns half the basements and barns in St Yzans and knows all the secrets, remembered everything best, but then he knows everything about everybody.

Everyone had a story about the meals they had had in the Ladra/Pautard house. Some had old photographs to share. I quickly got inspired to re-create some of those dishes.

By fall we had signed the deeds, toasted with Champagne, and were ready to start—with the kitchen, of course. We formed a small team, led by jack-of-all-trades Sasha, a Russian ex-soldier, not without charm and certainly not without temper, whose many talents as a handyman were overshadowed only by his gifts as a storyteller. He almost always does his job well—and when he doesn't, it's simply not his fault. Heat, cold, humidity, rain, and sun are all his allies. When Oddur asked in winter why the paint was peeling off the wall, Sasha replied, "Because you are not heating enough." When Oddur asked in summer why the paint was peeling off the wall,

Sasha said, "Because your house is too hot." An ex-bouncer at a pub near the beach, Sasha has an imposing presence, the build of a rugby player, and a German shepherd whose temperament matches that of his master. Sasha likes to talk of himself in the third person, and in the months when work had started but before we moved in, he gave himself much credit for deterring "thieves and gypsies." "Hah, none of those guys dares so much as look at the house with Sasha in the garden," he'd say, and then he would laugh like only he can and, at some point, quote his idol, Vladimir Putin.

Come November, Sasha's beautiful work in the kitchen was done, and I started using the room immediately. We'd sometimes come to the house on the weekends and I'd cook all day as if we lived there already. Then we'd pack up all the food and head back home to the forest. But a large family, no matter how much we love cooking, needs more than just a semifunctional kitchen, and Sasha's pace left me wondering if we'd ever move in. One day, Oddur drafted the men who were planting the olive trees outside to paint a few rooms so we could at least move in before Christmas.

Which is what we did, right on Christmas Eve. Oddur drove the move; no matter what, he was going to spend Christmas in the new house. So he dragged us and the dogs kicking and screaming in several car rides filled with presents and sheets and food until we had just enough stuff at No 1 rue de Loudenne to celebrate the holidays. You could call it adventurous. It was definitely hectic. I wasn't really up for it, but I allowed it to happen. And it was the best Christmas of my life.

FROM THE DAY I first set foot in No 1 rue de Loudenne, when I first walked into that beautiful big kitchen that I now cook in every day, when I discovered that the house had been a restaurant, when I realized that it had a big dining room and a second, smaller kitchen next to that, I knew what would happen next.

This was the house that had to be a restaurant and this is the book that wrote itself.

PLANTIA'S TARTE TATIN

~~~~~ SERVES 6 ~~~~~

I never got to meet Plantia, our house's former mistress, who lived in another era. But from having asked around and talked to villagers who remember her from when they were children, I know she was a woman with a deep love of food. Her cooking may not have been adventurous, but what she cooked was always of the highest standard with the finest produce around. Her absolute favorite dessert was a classic tarte Tatin, and she wouldn't serve it with crème fraîche for anything; it was all down to the caramelized apples. If they weren't good enough, she simply wouldn't make the tarte—maybe she'd settle for an apple compote instead. But when she approved of the apples, when she really wanted to make someone happy, she turned to her signature dessert.

It gives me goose bumps, cooking in this kitchen where I have also written this book, to think that a hundred years ago, another woman was cooking the very same thing in the very same corner, according to the same principles. Plantia, I promise I will never ever make a tarte Tatin without thinking of the lady in black.

FOR THE SWEET TART DOUGH

1½ CUPS / 180 G ALL-PURPOSE FLOUR, SIFTED, PLUS MORE FOR ROLLING

⅓ CUP / 65 G SUGAR

PINCH OF FINE SEA SALT

1 LARGE EGG YOLK

7 TABLESPOONS / 100 G COLD UNSALTED BUTTER, CUT INTO SMALL PIECES, PLUS MORE FOR THE PAN

1. **MAKE THE DOUGH.** Put the flour in a large bowl and make a well in the center. Add the sugar, salt, and egg yolk and mix slowly with your hands. Add the butter and mix well until you have a smooth and homogenous dough. Form it into a ball, cover with plastic wrap, and refrigerate for at least 1 hour or overnight.

2. Preheat the oven to 350°F / 180°C. Butter a 9-inch / 23 cm ovenproof skillet.

(recipe continues)

½ CUP / 100 G SUGAR

1 VANILLA BEAN, SPLIT
LENGTHWISE, SEEDS SCRAPED
AND RESERVED

6½ TABLESPOONS / 90 G UNSALTED
BUTTER, CUT INTO SMALL PIECES

2 POUNDS / 900 G APPLES, PEELED,
CORED, AND QUARTERED

CRÈME FRAÎCHE, FOR SERVING

3. **START THE APPLES.** Mix the sugar with the vanilla seeds. Sprinkle the vanilla sugar over the bottom of the skillet, scatter the butter over the sugar, and then tightly pack the apples in the pan in a circular fashion with one flat side down.

4. Put the pan on the stovetop over medium-high heat and cook until the liquid starts to bubble, about 3 minutes. Reduce the heat and continue to cook until the juices turn a golden caramel color, about 10 minutes. Remove from the heat.

5. On a lightly floured work surface, roll out the dough to a ⅛-inch / 3 mm thickness. Using a sharp knife, cut a round of dough just slightly larger than the top of the skillet. Drape the dough over the apples to cover and carefully use your fingers to tuck the dough between the pan and the apples on all sides.

6. Transfer to the oven and bake until the pastry is golden brown, about 40 minutes.

7. Let cool for 5 minutes. Wearing oven mitts or using kitchen towels, carefully (the caramel is hot) unmold by placing a large serving plate on top of the pan and inverting the cake onto the plate. Serve with crème fraîche.

A FAMILY RESTAURANT

A bird spreads his wings and flies over mountains, a hunting dog chases after a flock of deer in the forest, a child runs on a sandy beach flying a kite, an onion boils in a pot over a hot stove waiting to be transformed into a soup. Each is fulfilling its purpose, and though I'm not sure an onion can experience happiness, especially in a boiling pot, all of it feels right and how it should be when things, even the mundane, fall into place. But what about a house? Can a grand old house—rich with history, whose halls used to echo with laugher, fireplaces used to burn bright, and large rooms used to be filled with people eating delicious food—can that house ever be "happy" being just a family home? Won't a family, even one with nine people and many dogs, still make it feel less than full? Won't it think, "This is all very nice, but where are all the people?"

From that January day when I first set foot in No 1 rue de Loudenne, it has been clear to me that the house needed to awaken from its long slumber. We were looking for a family home, but we found something more, something bigger, more interesting, and in a strange way it felt like my duty to bring it all back to life. *How* was much less clear. I have always loved restaurants and spent a good deal of my life enjoying them. But running one myself? In a house that wasn't really ready, with a nonexistent staff—apart from my eager and very accommodating family? (And don't you need a license? And maybe a dishwasher?)

We decided to start small, hosting a few cooking workshops throughout the year, welcoming a few fresh faces every month to keep the house guessing. Class after class of like-minded food-loving, wine-drinking people made its way to this quiet town to spend hours eating and drinking. I was emboldened.

Then, true to form for us, we announced, perhaps a bit prematurely, that we'd also be opening a pop-up restaurant in the summer. Sasha, ever optimistic, said, "That's never going to happen." Then he paused and gestured that it might be possible, with more money of course. We formed a little team, with one member we quickly realized we couldn't live without, Allegra from Pescara, Italy, who stated on her application that she excels in scuba diving and used to play professional basketball—though her height does not suggest this (we later found out, when her father visited, that he had sponsored the team and even then she had had a hard time getting playing time).

When summer neared, I started getting serious jitters and would say to Oddur on a daily basis, "I'm not sure I can do this." But there was a little fire burning inside me that made me feel all along that somehow we would pull it off. Every morning (or sometimes in the afternoon) I saw Sasha disappear from the garden into the part of the house where we planned to have the restaurant. His face was usually not encouraging, though his expression tended to improve after a dozen coffees. Monsieur Bianco, the French/Italian plumber who prides himself on having 1,100 clients (making me number 1,101), was by July much more interested in talking about his impending holiday in Corsica than the toilets he was supposed to install days later. But we had already posted our opening date as Saturday, August 8. I still don't really know how we managed to make it all happen, to get Monsieur Bianco and Monsieur Simon, the electrician, to work in a very un-French way in the sacred month of August. Something tells me that Sasha, whose favorite mantra is that Russians will work on any day of the year, made them an offer they couldn't refuse.

A RESTAURANT is never more ready than the people who work there, and by the first week of August we weren't ready at all. April, a free-spirited world-wanderer and a butterfly of a friend, had announced her willingness to "work for food and shelter," and though I didn't know her well, I knew her well enough to know that she'd be a perfect fit. It was a mix of her experience and my intuition. I also needed help in the kitchen. Allegra would of course do her part, but she had so many other things on her plate, and our two eldest, Gunnhildur and Þórir, amazing as they are, hardly had the experience to cook in a restaurant. There was a week where I had nightmare visions of myself standing at the stove, cooking a four-course meal for thirty people without much help, and my husband's contribution would be, as ever, to "just stall them with another bottle of Champagne." The solution came in the unlikely form of a tattooed Brooklyn dude named Miles. My friend Yolanda had

recommended him to me, through a friendship with his mother, and this late in the game he would simply have to do. Miles was up for it (he always is), and after a part-frightening, part-encouraging phone conversation, I bought him a one-way ticket to Paris.

The leather aprons (our only staff uniform) arrived the day before opening but the white linen napkins didn't make it in time, forcing us to wash and iron every single piece of white cotton we could find in the house. Þórir, our eighteen-year-old, was assigned, along with his four Icelandic buddies who were visiting (yes, we were hosting a teenage army on top of everything), to fetch Miles at the train station. At least the house was clean and beautiful—every shelf, corner table, and buffet filled with fruits and flowers, silver polished. There were cases of wine ready to be opened, Champagne bursting with excitement in the fridge. In our cellar, we had pounds of duck from the butcher and crates of tomatoes from our vegetable garden. Allegra and I would man the cooking stations; Oddur, April, and Gunnhildur would charm and pour in the front room; and Hudson, our nine-year-old, would take care of the water—still or sparkling became his calling. His younger sisters Louise and Gaïa mainly got in the way, but, let's say, "with appeal." Notable absentees that night were Mia, who was in Spain for a holiday, and baby Audrey May, sleeping soundly in her bed.

We started with Champagne and radishes served with butter and salt and a selection of dried black pig sausages from my four-fingered butcher, Monsieur Manenti. Then we planned an amuse-bouche—a thick slice of foie gras served with figs that we had picked ourselves, or oysters, baked or raw (or, later, when Miles got "cheffy" on us, a langoustine crudo with cucumbers). The menu offered two choices for each of three courses: starter, main, and dessert.

That first night the room was filled with friends: Fabien, who had been instrumental in helping us find the house, and his wife, Flo; Linda and Jeffrey, who came for a workshop in March but ended up buying a house in St Yzans three days later (and who would throw their wedding dinner in the restaurant that summer); Anne and Michelle, the wonderful couple who run an antiques store in St Christoly and have supplied a large amount of our furniture. That night, among other dishes, we served a gazpacho made entirely from our tomatoes, a summer veal roast, and a walnut tart served with a small mountain of whipped cream. Of course there was, as always in this house, too much wine.

Sometime around midnight the Icelandic teenage team returned from the train station with Miles in tow. He looked much more like an out-of-it rock star than a reliable cook, and the first thing he said, when Oddur offered him a big glass of a 2000 Château Lynch-Bages, was, "This shit tastes like what we always have for my grandfather's birthday." Then he downed a few more glasses and got on with the party. I started wondering if flying him over had been such a good idea after all. I thought if he showed up the next morning at eight, it would be a minor miracle. (Fortunately, in St Yzans at least, miracles do happen.)

At the end of the night, Anne, who had perhaps been waiting with more anticipation for this than anyone, declared the evening *magique*.

THROUGHOUT AUGUST and into September the "*magique*" continued. Mostly it was all a big success, but there were a few moments of despair. Like that scorching hot day when the cream simply wouldn't whip and we opened pack after pack of heavy cream. Everyone in the kitchen had a theory. "It was the cream's fault, it should have been colder." "The bowl should be cold." "We should be less stressed"— as if the cream could sense our frustration. It all culminated in a scene in our little bathroom with the whole team up against an open window, Miles frantically rubbing the bowl with ice, April and Allegra taking turns whipping with a handheld machine, cream splattering in every direction. Not a pretty sight, but a funny one. At least one theory was tested beyond doubt during that lunch. Oddur's theory of just offering more wine. It always worked.

In that one month our clients were an interesting, international mix of readers of my blog, people who live in the region, and those who just wanted good food. There were date nights and family nights and even bring-your-child-with-you-to-date-night-and-put-him-to-sleep-in-a-separate-room-where-he-won't-disturb-us-but-probably-other-people nights. Every day Gunnhildur or Þórir or Oddur would bring us carefully curated crates of meats from my favorite butcher sources, fresh fish, and vegetables from local markets—especially from our organic farmer friends the Auberts—and, of course, from our own garden. Every day someone would drive the extra miles to Soulac-sur-Mer, about half an hour from our house, to get what we believe is the finest baguette in Médoc from a small, unassuming bakery called Le Fournil de J&J, run by the young couple behind the initials. Miles, Allegra, and I would then cook all this wonderful produce to the best of our abilities. April gradually improved her ironing, and by the end of it all I'd say we had gotten pretty good at "playing restaurant."

From time to time we had special guest appearances, like that starry night when Mr. Campari himself, the style editor of *Condé Nast Traveler* and now owner of

No 2 rue de Loudenne, mixed Negronis in what we call *la boucherie*—the butcher shop, our second "kitchen"—where guests entered and were served Champagne and other drinks. Meanwhile Rica, my editor at Clarkson Potter (who will have approved these lines if you are reading them), was taking orders in the dining room and marshaling the kitchen in a way that I could only dream of. Cyrille, her French chef husband, who usually presides over a kitchen staff of forty in New York, pitched in, too, directing Miles and Allegra, probably in a gentler way than he is used to. That same night we had two journalists from *House & Garden* who had come to interview me and were trying to do so over dinner, although soon they got much more interested in Matt's Negronis and all the wine that followed. We all ended up in the "*boucherie*" at midnight, opening more bottles of wine, turning what started as a proper restaurant earlier in the evening into a casual, kitchen after-party.

The guests who came to No 1 rue de Loudenne invariably turned into friends who would never leave, and I always took that as a compliment.

GOÛTER

EVERYDAY PEAR CAKE *39*

FAR BRETON *40*

OLD-FASHIONED ORANGE CAKE *43*

FIG *and* **PISTACHIO CAKE** *44*

GÂTEAU BRETON *49*

APPLE PANCAKES *50*

CINNAMON CRÊPES *with* **CREAM**
and **STRAWBERRIES** *52*

BRIOCHE *55*

BEIGNETS *with* **APRICOT FILLING** *56*

I'M VERY FOND OF ICONIC THINGS. And France has such a wealth of them—many of which revolve around food. The plump, mustachioed gourmand at the brasserie enjoying frogs' legs and a bottle of wine. The *monsieur* sipping a *ballon de rouge* before noon at the corner café. The "mothers" of Lyon, cooking delicious but simple food in their own restaurants. My favorite images, though, just might be the ones with children—children and pastry, to be specific. The little girl in a red coat, strolling through the park on her way home from school, carrying her schoolbag in one hand, a crêpe with salted-butter caramel in the other, perhaps stopping along the way for a quick ride on the carousel.

In France we have, like everybody else, breakfast, lunch, and dinner. But we also have something else, something sacred: *l'heure du goûter*, a special hour that involves kids and cakes and usually comes right after school. The reward for a long day in the classroom is stopping by the local *boulangerie*, waiting in line with the other kids and their parents, scanning the treats displayed in the glass case, and picking out a favorite.

On weekends this sacred hour often takes on elevated status; instead of going to the *boulangerie*, all the action is in the family kitchen where someone (probably mom but more recently also dad) will be baking something simple but always delicious and special. The kids often (and always in *this* house) get to participate in the baking. For them, messing around in the kitchen is half the fun. These recipes will be some of the first ones they learn to make on their own, by heart, and will someday teach to their children.

What follows are moments of true family bliss, children seated around the kitchen table, savoring every bite of their afternoon treats, with a glass of milk or a cup of deep, dark hot chocolate with a dollop of whipped cream.

And by children, of course, I mean children of all ages.

EVERYDAY PEAR CAKE

⁓ SERVES 6 TO 8 ⁓

This has been my husband's favorite cake for many years, and as a result I make it often. When we get used to doing something, we tend to say we could do it blindfolded, but in all seriousness, I think I could make this cake in my sleep. This pear cake falls into the category of desserts Oddur likes that are not too sweet and that he'd happily have with or without cream, or even crème fraîche. It seems that food preferences are genetic, because once when my father-in-law was staying with us, he finished a whole cake by himself. I remember having a lot of ripe pears (which are the best to use for this cake; a pear is never better than just before it goes bad), and so I made two cakes for the family. I was expecting to have some left over for breakfast the following day, which works very well with this cake. But my father-in-law had other plans: We had one cake; he had the other one. He did it very discreetly, cutting slice after slice until there was nothing left. This simple cake does that to people.

3 LARGE EGGS

¾ CUP / 150 G GRANULATED SUGAR

1¼ CUPS / 150 G ALL-PURPOSE FLOUR, SIFTED

¼ CUP / 30 G CORNSTARCH

1 TEASPOON BAKING POWDER

PINCH OF FINE SEA SALT

½ TEASPOON VANILLA EXTRACT

6½ TABLESPOONS / 90 G UNSALTED BUTTER, MELTED

4 TO 5 RIPE MEDIUM PEARS, PEELED AND CUT INTO CHUNKS

CONFECTIONERS' SUGAR, FOR SERVING

1. Preheat the oven to 350°F / 180°C. Line the bottom of a 9-inch / 23 cm springform pan with parchment paper.

2. In a large bowl, whisk together the eggs and granulated sugar until light in color and fluffy.

3. In a medium bowl, sift together the flour, cornstarch, baking powder, and salt. Whisk into the egg mixture, followed by the vanilla and melted butter. Fold in the pears with their juices.

4. Pour the batter into the prepared pan and bake until golden and a knife inserted in the center comes out clean, about 45 minutes. Cool in the pan on a wire rack for 5 minutes before unmolding and peeling away the parchment paper.

5. Serve warm or at room temperature, sprinkled with confectioners' sugar.

FAR BRETON

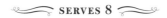

I often get an intense craving for this simple custardy cake. It's not really a seasonal thing: Prunes, rum, and milk are always available. It usually happens like this: I'm alone in the kitchen, children at school or napping, Oddur somewhere else, probably walking the dogs. Then it hits me: I must make a *far breton*, for the kids, for me. The ingredients are always on hand so all I have to do is drench the prunes in rum and wait. The clock is ticking because soon the kids will be home from school, and I love being the *maman* who welcomes them with a freshly baked treat. Hearing little voices in the alley behind the house that leads to the kitchen back door is my favorite moment. The first child enters, and then one, often Hudson, will recognize the smell and a little smile will break out on his face. He loves rum in cakes like I do (which I hope is not a bad thing), and seconds later they are all seated around the kitchen table having a glass of milk and warm *far breton*. That's when life is a little bit perfect.

2 CUPS / 300 G PITTED PRUNES

½ CUP / 120 ML DARK RUM

3¼ CUPS / 760 ML WHOLE MILK

⅔ CUP / 130 G SUGAR

1 VANILLA BEAN, SPLIT
LENGTHWISE, SEEDS SCRAPED
AND RESERVED

4 LARGE EGGS

PINCH OF FINE SEA SALT

1¾ CUPS PLUS 2 TABLESPOONS /
225 G ALL-PURPOSE FLOUR, SIFTED

1 TEASPOON SALTED BUTTER, PLUS
MORE FOR THE DISH

1. In a small bowl, combine the prunes and rum and set aside for at least 2 hours so the prunes soak up the rum. Reserving the rum, drain the prunes. Set aside separately.

2. Preheat the oven to 400°F / 200°C. Grease a 7 × 11-inch / 18 × 28 cm baking dish.

3. In a saucepan, bring the milk, sugar, and vanilla bean and seeds to a simmer over medium heat.

4. Meanwhile, in a large bowl, beat together the eggs and salt.

5. Discard the vanilla pod and slowly pour the warm milk into the eggs, whisking constantly. Pour in the reserved rum and continue to whisk. Gradually whisk in the flour.

6. Pour half of the batter into the prepared dish. Scatter the prunes evenly in the dish and then pour in the remaining batter. Transfer to the oven and bake for 30 minutes.

7. Reduce the oven temperature to 350°F / 180°C. Remove the *far* from the oven and gently spread the butter on top. Return to the oven until the *far* is set in the center, about 10 minutes. Let cool completely on a wire rack before cutting into pieces and serving.

OLD-FASHIONED ORANGE CAKE

 SERVES 8

Alot of my cooking is based on abundance, on what's most in season: fava beans in April, peaches in July, pumpkins in October. This cake is the opposite, at least in my mind. I like to imagine a time when not everyone could get oranges all the time. A family gets an unexpected gift, maybe from a stranger, as a thank-you for a good deed: a crate of the most beautiful, juiciest oranges. They open a few and feast on them; it's all very special. Then someone in the family, the one who is best at baking, decides to bake an orange cake. This is a great occasion, the event of the week. They talk about the cake for days, and then one day heavenly aromas fill the kitchen, the cake is ready, and the family gathers to eat it. The best cake they've ever had, so moist, so wonderfully perfumed with oranges. It feels like Christmas, and maybe it is.

15 TABLESPOONS / 210 G UNSALTED BUTTER, MELTED, PLUS MORE FOR THE PAN

1¼ CUPS / 150 G ALL-PURPOSE FLOUR

2 TEASPOONS BAKING POWDER

½ TEASPOON FINE SEA SALT

2 ORANGES, PREFERABLY ORGANIC

3 LARGE EGGS

1 CUP PLUS 2 TABLESPOONS / 225 G SUGAR

¼ CUP / 60 ML ORANGE LIQUEUR

1. Preheat the oven to 350°F / 180°C. Grease a Bundt cake pan with butter.

2. In a medium bowl, sift together the flour, baking powder, and salt.

3. Peel one of the oranges, cut into chunks, and purée in a food processor.

4. In a large bowl, whisk together the eggs and sugar until light in color and fluffy. Mix in the puréed orange. Fold in the flour mixture and then mix in the melted butter and orange liqueur.

5. Pour the batter into the prepared pan. Bake until golden brown and a knife inserted into the cake comes out clean, 40 to 50 minutes. Let cool in the pan on a wire rack for 5 minutes before unmolding and letting cool completely.

6. Before serving, using a citrus zester, zest the remaining orange and scatter the zest all over the cake.

FIG AND PISTACHIO CAKE

⥽ SERVES 6 ⥼

This is my garden party cake, the one I'd make if the Queen of England ever came to visit. She'd have to come in fig season, of course, and we'd have tea and a slice each of this moist cake. We would sit there and discuss our dogs, and she would comment that fox terriers have a terrible reputation and that, in her opinion, corgis are a much more interesting breed. She's the Queen so I wouldn't argue with that; afterward we'd just stick to the weather and have more cake.

8 TABLESPOONS / 120 G UNSALTED BUTTER, PLUS MORE FOR THE PAN

1⅓ CUPS / 200 G UNSALTED PISTACHIOS, PLUS MORE FOR GARNISH

¾ CUP / 150 G SUGAR

1 TEASPOON VANILLA EXTRACT

6 LARGE EGG YOLKS

6 LARGE EGG WHITES

PINCH OF FINE SEA SALT

½ CUP / 120 ML HEAVY CREAM

¼ CUP / 60 ML MASCARPONE CHEESE

2 TABLESPOONS HONEY, PLUS MORE FOR DRIZZLING

2 TABLESPOONS ORANGE FLOWER WATER

10 SMALL FRESH FIGS, QUARTERED

1. Preheat the oven to 350°F / 180°C. Grease an 8-inch / 20 cm cake pan with butter.

2. In a food processor, combine the pistachios, butter, ½ cup / 100 g of the sugar, and the vanilla and pulse for a minute or until you get a smooth paste. Add the egg yolks, one by one, and pulse until well combined. Transfer the pistachio mixture to a large bowl.

3. Using an electric mixer, whip the egg whites, and when the mixture starts to foam, add the salt. Continue to whip on high speed, gradually adding the remaining ¼ cup / 50 g sugar, until the whites hold stiff peaks. Fold the egg whites into the pistachio mixture.

4. Pour the batter into the prepared pan and bake until a knife inserted in the center comes out clean, about 25 minutes. Let cool in the pan for 10 minutes before unmolding onto a wire rack to cool completely.

5. Using an electric mixer, whip together the heavy cream, mascarpone, honey, and orange flower water until the cream holds stiff peaks, about 3 minutes.

6. Spread the cream on top of the cooled cake and arrange the quartered figs on top. Crush some pistachios and scatter all over. Finish with a drizzle of honey to gloss it up. Serve immediately.

EPICERIE FINE
Plaisirs Gourmands

GÂTEAU BRETON

SERVES 6

Brittany may be the region in France where they make the best desserts. Other regions have delicious little confections and pastries, but I can't think of any other region that has so many good ones. The Bretons have a secret weapon, butter, and they are not afraid to use it. Their desserts may look a little ordinary—in fact, Breton desserts are the polar opposite of sumptuous frosted cakes that look the part—but they never taste it. I challenge you not to finish this buttery cake the day you make it; if you can resist, it is even better the next day.

16 TABLESPOONS / 225 G SALTED
BUTTER, AT ROOM TEMPERATURE,
PLUS MORE FOR THE PAN

3¼ CUPS / 390 G ALL-PURPOSE
FLOUR

1¼ CUPS / 250 G SUGAR

7 LARGE EGG YOLKS

2 TABLESPOONS DARK RUM

1 VANILLA BEAN, SPLIT
LENGTHWISE, SEEDS SCRAPED
AND RESERVED

1 TABLESPOON WHOLE MILK

1. Preheat the oven to 350°F / 180°C. Butter a 9-inch / 23 cm cake pan.

2. In a large bowl, mix together the flour and sugar. Make a well in the center and add 6 of the egg yolks to it. Mix together the ingredients with your hands, gradually incorporating the butter, rum, and vanilla seeds.

3. When the dough is smooth, shape it into a round about 9 inches / 23 cm in diameter. Transfer it to the prepared pan and flatten with the palms of your hands to fill the pan evenly.

4. In a small bowl, mix the remaining egg yolk with the milk. Brush the cake with the egg wash and use a fork to score decorative lines on top of the cake.

5. Bake until the cake is golden brown and a knife inserted in the center comes out clean, about 35 minutes. Let cool in the pan for 10 minutes before unmolding. Serve warm or at room temperature.

APPLE PANCAKES

SERVES 8

Pescajoune come from the region in the South of France where my mother grew up; my aunt used to make them for me as a kid. Originally from the Quercy province of France, *pescajounes* are pancakes filled with fruit. My children, especially the younger ones, enjoy making these with me, so I let them prepare the batter and put in the apples, and then I do all the frying. This is Sunday fare, quite healthy as I include buckwheat in the batter, and I think you can never have too many apples in your diet. This is also the recipe that the bigger kids favor when they want to surprise me with breakfast in bed.

1¼ CUPS / 150 G BUCKWHEAT FLOUR

¾ CUP / 90 G ALL-PURPOSE FLOUR

1 TEASPOON BAKING POWDER

2 TABLESPOONS SUGAR

PINCH OF FINE SEA SALT

1¼ CUPS / 300 ML WHOLE MILK

5 LARGE EGG YOLKS

4 TABLESPOONS / 60 G UNSALTED BUTTER, MELTED, PLUS MORE FOR COOKING

2 TABLESPOONS DARK RUM

5 LARGE EGG WHITES

3 APPLES, PEELED AND THINLY SLICED

CONFECTIONERS' SUGAR, FOR SERVING

1. Preheat the oven to 250°F / 120°C.

2. In a large bowl, sift together the buckwheat flour, all-purpose flour, and baking powder. Whisk in the sugar and salt, followed by the milk and egg yolks. Whisk in the melted butter and rum. The batter should be on the thick side.

3. Using an electric mixer, whip the egg whites until they hold stiff peaks. Fold the egg whites into the batter, followed by the sliced apples.

4. In a large sauté pan or on a griddle, melt some butter over medium-high heat. Working in batches, add about 2 tablespoons of the batter for each 4- to 5-inch / 10 to 12.5 cm pancake. Cook until golden brown, about 2 minutes per side. Transfer to a baking sheet and keep warm in the oven while you continue to make pancakes with the remaining batter. Serve warm with confectioners' sugar.

CINNAMON CRÊPES WITH CREAM AND STRAWBERRIES

This is a recipe from my Icelandic mother-in-law, Jóhanna. She's been making these crêpes forever, always in the same pan, and when she comes to stay with us she brings the pan with her. It's a very popular recipe in Iceland, perfect for long, dark days when there is nothing better than to snuggle up inside and watch the weather blowing outside. Jóhanna always makes a lot of crêpes: The first twenty-five are eaten immediately by the army of children waiting impatiently next to the stove. The next twenty-five she lets cool slightly before folding them over a generous portion of whipped cream, sometimes with strawberries. They are divine, so much so that I started making them, too, though Jóhanna's remain better than mine. There is a story involved that I'm not sure I should go into (you know, mothers-in-law, and all that), but here goes: When Oddur, my husband, was little he never really liked these crêpes (much to his mother's chagrin), particularly not the ones with cream. But now he's developed a fondness for them, even the creamy ones. This irritates Jóhanna, and when she sees him eating them she just shakes her head. He tries to explain that he's just grown into them but she won't have any of it . . . mothers and sons.

2 TABLESPOONS / 30 G UNSALTED BUTTER

⅓ CUP / 65 G SUGAR

2 LARGE EGGS

2 CUPS / 500 ML WHOLE MILK

½ TEASPOON VANILLA EXTRACT

1½ CUPS / 180 G ALL-PURPOSE FLOUR

1½ TEASPOONS GROUND CINNAMON

1 TEASPOON BAKING POWDER

¼ TEASPOON FINE SEA SALT

1 CUP / 250 ML HEAVY CREAM

STRAWBERRIES, DICED

1. In a small (8-inch / 20 cm) sauté pan over medium heat, melt the butter. Remove from the heat and set aside to cool.

2. In a large bowl, whisk together the sugar and eggs for a minute. Gradually whisk in the milk and vanilla. In a separate bowl, whisk together the flour, cinnamon, baking powder, and salt. Whisk the flour mixture into the milk mixture until you get a smooth, fluid batter. Finally, stir in the melted butter.

3. Return the sauté pan to medium-high heat. When the pan is very hot, spoon 2 tablespoons of the batter into the pan, swirling the pan to cover the surface evenly. Cook for a minute or so, until the edges start browning. Lift the edges slightly with a butter knife, then flip the crêpe and brown the other side, about 30 seconds.

4. Transfer the crêpe to a plate and continue cooking the remaining batter in the same fashion, stacking the crêpes on top of one another. You should get 20 to 25 crêpes. When finished, cover the stack with an inverted plate, wrap in a clean kitchen towel, and cover with plastic wrap or a plastic bag to keep the crêpes moist and soft. You can keep them this way for up to 6 hours before serving.

5. Just before serving, whip the cream until it holds soft peaks. Spoon a tablespoon or so of whipped cream into the center of each crêpe, add some diced strawberries, and then fold in half and in half again to form a triangle. Serve immediately.

BRIOCHE

When we lived in Paris, Oddur would always take the dogs for a walk in the early hours and return with a fresh baguette, some croissants, and, if I was lucky and he had gone to my favorite bakery, freshly baked brioche. Depending on the day, the brioche would either be individual little ones with the cute hats or a larger loaf that we'd slice. Either way, we'd always have it with a selection of jams and butter. I'd have my favorite tea (French breakfast tea infused with vanilla and chocolate) and stay in bed as long as possible. Here in Médoc, fantastic brioche is harder to come by, and you have to go farther to find it. Which means I have to make my own. Once in a blue moon on the weekend, I'll wake up extra early and bake a treat for the whole family. It's a lovely thing to do, but because I love staying in bed, this brioche often ends up being an afternoon treat rather than a gorgeous breakfast. No one seems to mind.

1 ENVELOPE (¼ OUNCE / 7 G) ACTIVE DRY YEAST

2 TABLESPOONS LUKEWARM WATER

2¾ CUPS / 300 G ALL-PURPOSE FLOUR, SIFTED, PLUS MORE FOR KNEADING

¼ CUP / 50 G GRANULATED SUGAR

PINCH OF FINE SEA SALT

6½ TABLESPOONS / 90 G UNSALTED BUTTER, CUBED, AT ROOM TEMPERATURE, PLUS MORE FOR THE PAN

3 LARGE EGGS

⅓ CUP / 90 ML WHOLE MILK, SLIGHTLY WARMED

2 TABLESPOONS ORANGE FLOWER WATER

A HANDFUL OF PEARL SUGAR (OPTIONAL)

note
I use a traditional brioche mold, but you can really use any pan you wish, such as a deep cake pan or a loaf pan.

1. In a small bowl, dissolve the yeast in the lukewarm water. Set aside until frothy, 5 to 10 minutes.

2. In a large bowl, mix together the flour, granulated sugar, salt, yeast mixture, and butter. Gradually add 2 of the eggs followed by the milk and orange flower water and mix well with a big wooden spoon. Turn the dough out onto a lightly floured surface and start kneading until you get a smooth ball of dough, 8 to 10 minutes. Cover the bowl with a cloth and let the dough rise in a warm room overnight.

3. Start kneading the dough on an unfloured surface, just to get rid of a few trapped air bubbles, 1 to 2 minutes. Shape back into a ball. Grease an 8-inch / 20 cm brioche mold (see Note) generously with butter and put the dough inside. Cover with a cloth and let it rise again for 1 to 2 hours (depending on how patient you are!).

4. Preheat the oven to 350°F / 180°C.

5. Lightly beat the remaining egg. Using a brush, glaze the surface of the brioche with the beaten egg. Sprinkle the pearl sugar on top (if using). Bake the brioche until risen and golden brown, about 40 minutes. If the top starts to brown too much, place a sheet of parchment paper over it to protect it. Unmold and cool completely on a wire rack.

BEIGNETS WITH APRICOT FILLING

I've been making all sorts of beignets and *bugnes* for years, but this is one of the newer recipes in my repertoire. It's without a doubt one of the recipes that I enjoyed making most this year, even with the deep-frying and the relative mess it makes, because this recipe practically got a standing ovation from the family on its debut. When apricots are in season, this is a chic little treat with coffee at the end of a meal. For a special occasion or a special person, this is the recipe I recommend. Heavenly puffy pillows.

FOR THE BEIGNET DOUGH

1 ENVELOPE (¼ OUNCE / 7 G)
ACTIVE DRY YEAST

¾ CUP / 180 ML LUKEWARM WATER

4 CUPS / 480 G ALL-PURPOSE
FLOUR, SIFTED, PLUS MORE FOR
KNEADING

½ TEASPOON FINE SEA SALT

1 LARGE EGG, BEATEN

2 TABLESPOONS / 30 G UNSALTED
BUTTER, AT ROOM TEMPERATURE

¼ CUP / 50 G GRANULATED SUGAR

1 TEASPOON VANILLA EXTRACT

½ CUP / 120 ML EVAPORATED MILK

FOR THE FILLING

½ POUND / 225 G APRICOTS,
HALVED AND PITTED

¼ CUP / 50 G GRANULATED SUGAR

1 TABLESPOON ORANGE
FLOWER WATER

VEGETABLE OIL, FOR DEEP-FRYING

CONFECTIONERS' SUGAR,
FOR SERVING

1. **MAKE THE BEIGNET DOUGH.** In a small bowl, dissolve the yeast in ¼ cup / 60 ml of the warm water. Let it sit for about 5 minutes.

2. In a large bowl, mix the flour and salt and make a well in the center. Add the yeast mixture to the well and start to incorporate it into the flour. Gradually add and incorporate the egg, butter, granulated sugar, and vanilla. Pour the remaining ½ cup / 120 ml warm water over the mixture, mix it in, and then gradually mix in the evaporated milk. Turn the dough out onto a lightly floured surface and start kneading until the dough becomes soft and supple, 10 to 15 minutes. Shape into a ball. Lightly oil a clean bowl, add the dough, and cover with plastic wrap. Let rise until doubled in volume, 1 to 2 hours.

3. **MEANWHILE, MAKE THE FILLING.** In a medium saucepan, combine the apricots, granulated sugar, orange flower water, and 3 tablespoons water in a medium saucepan. Bring to a low boil over medium-low heat. Reduce the heat and continue to simmer until the apricots are soft, about 15 minutes. Purée the compote until smooth, preferably using an immersion blender. Set aside to cool. The compote will keep for several days in a glass jar in the refrigerator.

4. Refrigerate the risen dough for at least 30 minutes before rolling. Fill a pastry bag fitted with a small plain tip with the apricot compote.

5. On a floured surface, roll the dough to a ⅛-inch / 3 mm thickness. With a pastry wheel or knife, cut into 3-inch / 7.5 cm squares.

6. Pour 2 inches / 5 cm of vegetable oil into a large pot and heat over medium heat to 325°F / 160°C. Test the temperature of the oil by dropping in a small piece of dough. If the dough turns golden within seconds, the oil is ready.

7. Working in batches, fry the dough squares in the oil until golden and puffy, a few seconds or so on each side. Remove with a slotted spoon and drain on paper towels.

8. Poke the pastry tip into the side of each warm beignet and inject some apricot compote into the center of each beignet. Sprinkle with confectioners' sugar. Serve immediately.

⚬—⚬ THE IMPORTANCE OF L'APÉRO ⚬—⚬

THE BEFORE, THE DURING, AND THE AFTER. The Americans, masters of marketing, invented happy hour and commercialized the cocktail. But the French had already been there years before with *l'apéritif*, where no happiness was required but there were undeniably better snacks. It's a philosophical question: Which of the eternal triumvirate of the before, the during, and the after is the most important? The "during" stakes a convincing claim in my book, but what would we ever do in France without the before: the all-important *apéro*?

Other cultures have their own version of *l'apéro*, but I think the French do it best. And why is that? Because the food is better would be my answer. They also keep the drinks simple, not too much mixing and shaking. The English have their port (which I love) or their Scotch (which I don't), the Americans their cocktails (which I love a little bit), but the French have their drinks —often Champagne or perhaps a kir (white wine with a splash of crème de cassis)—*with* a little something, a nibble, whether oysters or radishes and butter or charcuterie or some combination. It's that little something that makes all the difference in *l'heure de l'apéro*.

CHAMPAGNE

Champagne is the most important drink in France. It's what we use to celebrate the good days, landmark days, and, sometimes, regular days when we just want some Champagne. It goes with pretty much everything and is a great opener to anything. It's the first thing I order in any restaurant and the last thing I will ever give up.

Once, in a store in Bordeaux that sells only Champagne, I met a chic little man who was buying a considerable number of bottles—from various makers and of various standing. He explained to me that while Champagne will always be Champagne, there are different ones for different occasions. He always has a few bottles in his fridge and a few cases in his *cave*. If good friends arrive unexpectedly, he opens a nice one—but not too nice. It's not, he elaborated, that they don't deserve the best, but going for the really fine Champagne would be ostentatious for an impromptu visit, and one should never show off. Then there is the really good Champagne. That's reserved for when he hosts a formal soirée or dinner. Finally there is the very grand, very old Champagne that he will never drink, because no occasion will ever be good enough.

The French and their Champagne.

TWO (ITALIAN) APÉRITIFS

The following two drinks are admittedly Italian rather than French, but they have become part of our family's *apéritif* repertoire . . . because we often holiday in Italy, because we always have a lot of peaches, and because one of our friends loves to make Negronis. Besides, by now these drinks are truly international and can be ordered in many French cafés and bars.

HUDSON'S BELLINI

SERVES 10

My son, Hudson, is a budding businessman with an eye for any opportunity to make a few francs. A few summers ago his father (who is not really a business-man but rather a first-class bon vivant) taught him how to make Bellinis, a favorite summer *apéritif*. My son soon realized that serving free Bellinis to his father wasn't going to get him anywhere and maybe there were better opportunities elsewhere. Every year I'm asked to participate in various fairs and festivals around Médoc, to cook something or say something, and I always try to. One summer, at the biggest fair of the year in nearby St Christoly, we had a family stand where we were selling chanterelle tartlets (see the recipe on page 94) and the younger girls were selling lemonade. Hudson set up shop next to them, and for every lemonade they sold he sold about ten Bellinis, at a much higher price. I told him to be nice to his sisters, so he went and used some of his profits to buy a roast chicken at a stall close by. Then he ate most of it himself.

8 TO 10 RIPE WHITE PEACHES, PEELED

1 BOTTLE (750 ML) PROSECCO, CHILLED

SPARKLING WATER, CHILLED

1. Squeeze the peaches by hand (a must) into a container. Use a strainer to filter the pulp, so you'll end up with a thick juice. You will have a generous 2 cups / 500 ml. Refrigerate until cold.

2. Pour into each Champagne glass 2 parts peach juice and 3 parts Prosecco. Top with a splash of sparkling water.

3. For children, skip the Prosecco and add more sparkling water. Sell for half price.

MATT'S NEGRONI

SERVES 1

Soon after we bought our house in St Yzans, our friends from Brooklyn, Matt and Yolanda, bought two houses opposite us. I guess they have always had one eye on retiring in France, and when they are done with their high-flying magazine jobs in New York, we can all go looking for mushrooms together. Matt is a keen hunter, keen dresser, and, maybe most of all, a cocktail connoisseur. His specialty: the Negroni. They spend their summers in St Yzans and were, of course, here for the restaurant. Yolanda drank the Champagne, did some dishes. Matt mainly plundered our pantry. One special night in August, one of our biggest, we asked him to make Negronis for the guests, and he obliged—which meant he had to compete with the Champagne. Always the salesman, Matt made sure that everybody had a Negroni, then Champagne, then . . . That was the night we all ended up in the *boucherie* opening countless bottles of wine.

1 PART GIN (MATT LIKES LONDON DRY)

1 PART SWEET VERMOUTH (MATT LIKES PUNT E MES)

1 PART CAMPARI

1 ORANGE SLICE

Put one or two very large ice cubes in an old-fashioned glass, add the gin, vermouth, and Campari, and stir to combine. Garnish with the orange slice and serve immediately.

RHUBARB AND RASPBERRY CORDIAL

MAKES 1 CUP / 240 ML

Cooking with rhubarb has never really come that easily to me. I usually make a compote that goes well with creamy desserts like panna cotta, and Gunnhildur, our eldest, makes a lovely Icelandic rhubarb pudding. I've also made a pretty good rhubarb crumble. But other than that I haven't been very adventurous with it. In spite of this, we often seem to have a lot of rhubarb in our house, whether from the market, where it looks fresh and healthy, or from our vegetable garden, where it seems to thrive. At some point during the summer I'll have a small rhubarb problem, and two summers ago I found a solution. A cordial is a light, fizzy, fruity summer drink that pretty much beats any other on a scorching hot day in July. I often get the kids to help me make it, which they enjoy, and then we sip it together on the rooftop terrace in late afternoon. You can of course cheat a little and add sparkling wine to the cordial for *l'apéro*. But that's only for adults.

5 RHUBARB STALKS, CUT INTO
SMALL CHUNKS

5 OUNCES / 150 G RASPBERRIES

1 CUP / 200 G SUGAR

GRATED ZEST AND JUICE OF
2 SMALL LEMONS

SPARKLING WATER

A LARGE HANDFUL OF FRESH
MINT LEAVES

1. In a large saucepan, combine the rhubarb, half of the raspberries, the sugar, lemon zest and juice, and ⅔ cup / 160 ml water. Bring to a low boil over medium heat, then reduce the heat and simmer until the rhubarb is tender and the consistency of the mixture is smooth, about 20 minutes. Strain through a sieve into a glass jar or bottle. Let cool completely and then refrigerate until cold. Covered, the cordial will keep for up to 5 days in the refrigerator.

2. Mix as much cordial as you like, depending on your taste, in a big carafe with sparkling water and ice cubes, garnishing with the remaining raspberries and some mint leaves. Serve immediately.

. . . AND THE SLIGHTLY LESS IMPORTANT DIGESTIF

Once my husband bought an architect's table at an antiques fair in Bordeaux. I asked him what he wanted to do with it. He had no idea. When the harvest room, where we had the restaurant, was ready, he simply put the table in one corner. He still had no idea what to do with it.

Then one day he had an epiphany. He bought about twenty old carafes and filled them with the finest Cognacs, Armagnacs, and whiskeys. He did it because he thought it looked good. It proved to be a good investment. When we have guests, when we have workshops, and during our restaurant weeks, that table is a source of conversation and intrigue. As our sommelier, he always hinted and gestured that a few lucky guests might be in for a treat.

By then he had forgotten which drink was in which bottle, but his nose could still tell the differences between the after-dinner spirits. I witnessed it a few times: He'd lead guests to the table and allow them to choose. They'd always ask for the best. And they always got the best, no matter which bottle they chose.

STARTERS

TOMATO GAZPACHO *72*

PLANTIA'S ONION SOUP *77*

LOBSTER BISQUE *78*

SIMPLE VEGETABLE POTAGE *80*

CELERY ROOT VELOUTÉ *83*

VICHYSSOISE *84*

PLANTIA'S SPRING
VEGETABLE STEW *86*

CHESTNUT *and* POTATO
GALETTES *91*

CHANTERELLE *and* GARLIC
TARTLETS *94*

POTATO CROQUETTES *with*
BAYONNE HAM *97*

PEARL ONION TARTES TATIN *100*

POTATO *and* CHARD GALETTES *103*

PUMPKIN QUICHE *with* BACON *104*

PUFF PASTRY SHELLS *with*
LANGOUSTINES *and* SCALLOPS *107*

BUTTERNUT PANCAKES
with SAGE BROWN BUTTER *108*

WHITE ASPARAGUS
SOUFFLÉ *112*

WILD MUSHROOMS
with an EGG YOLK *113*

SPRING FLAN *with* ZUCCHINI
and MINT *117*

BROILED OYSTERS *with*
FOIE GRAS *and*
SAUTERNES *118*

CHICKEN *and* LEMON PÂTÉ
EN CROÛTE *122*

ROAST BONE MARROW
with HERBS *125*

COUNTRY TERRINE *126*

FOR SOME REASON a lot of people seem to be unclear about exactly what French food is. While they seem pretty certain (though are not always correct) about, say, Chinese food, Indian food, and Italian food, French food seems to remain a mystery. Many are familiar with the clichés, like escargots and frogs' legs, oysters and onion soup, but they don't always know what makes a dish French. How is a steak French, for example? What do you have to do to it to make it so? And French fries, aren't they sort of American by now? Maybe a recipe is French if you put enough butter and cream into it, and wine? Maybe it's all about the sauce?

France is a country with many regions, and though its cuisine is not as localized as in Italy, where the country wasn't really united until recently, France has some strong regional specialties that make this question even harder to answer. In some ways you could say that Paris has played a key part in what the world sees as French cuisine. Historically, if someone tasted something delicious somewhere in France, the King and his court would probably want to have it. Someone would always, in the end, bring the recipe to the capital—and then others would want to try it, too.

Of course, there have been outside influences, too, like couscous from North Africa and oranges from Spain. And we aren't immune to fads: Nouvelle cuisine in the eighties introduced inventive pairings and teeny tiny portions that would never have been a match for the appetites of old. (Balzac, legend has it, used to scoff down two hundred oysters when he finished a book.)

To me, French food is what I like from the whole country, and though living in one (rather remote) region emphasizes certain things, like game and oysters and grilling over grapevine branches, I like to include recipes from all of France in my cooking. There is just so much good food, so many good techniques and traditions, and I never want to miss out on any of them.

And so I seek out the best possible seasonal ingredients, cook them thoughtfully and often simply (yes, frequently with butter and wine and garlic), eat just enough to satisfy myself, drink wines to complement my meal, and never count calories. Roast chicken with French fries could be made anywhere, but a really juicy one, perfectly seasoned, with the crispiest fries and the tastiest sauce, was invented in France, and I believe that, at least on a good day, nobody does it better.

TOMATO GAZPACHO

~ SERVES 4 TO 6 ~

For the last two years we have been growing our own tomatoes in the little vegetable garden down the road from our house. We have experimented with several different varieties: small cherry tomatoes for my veal stew and for casual bruschetta, ripe green and yellow tomatoes that are great in salads. But my favorite is the deep red, meaty, *coeur de boeuf* that tastes so much better than anything you can buy in stores. I love slicing a big juicy one, giving it a generous glug of good olive oil, sprinkling it with fleur de sel, and savoring it. They also make excellent gazpacho. While I used to make gazpacho with cucumbers and peppers in addition to the tomatoes, when you have really, really good tomatoes, you don't need anything more, only a little bread for substance and some garlic to spice everything up.

FOR THE GARNISH

½ CUP / 120 ML HEAVY CREAM

2 GARLIC CLOVES, MINCED

1 TABLESPOON EXTRA-VIRGIN
OLIVE OIL, PLUS MORE FOR SERVING

12 THIN SLICES BAGUETTE

FINE SEA SALT

FOR THE SOUP

1½ CUPS / 115 G CRUMBLED STALE
WHITE BREAD

2 POUNDS / 900 G VERY RIPE
TOMATOES, DICED

2 GARLIC CLOVES, SMASHED
AND PEELED

⅔ CUP / 150 ML EXTRA-VIRGIN
OLIVE OIL

1 TABLESPOON SHERRY VINEGAR

FINE SEA SALT AND FRESHLY
GROUND BLACK PEPPER

¼ TEASPOON PIMENT D'ESPELETTE
OR MILD CHILE POWDER,
FOR SERVING

1. **MAKE THE GARNISH.** In a small bowl, whisk together the cream and minced garlic. Cover with plastic wrap and chill in the refrigerator for at least 1 hour. Just before serving, pass the cream through a fine-mesh sieve, pressing on the garlic to release all its flavor.

2. In a large sauté pan, heat the olive oil over medium heat and cook the slices of bread until golden, about 30 seconds per side. Drain the croutons on a paper towel. Season with salt.

3. **MAKE THE SOUP.** Soak the bread in a bowl of cool water for 10 minutes, then drain, and squeeze out as much water as possible.

4. In a large bowl, combine the bread, tomatoes, garlic cloves, olive oil, and vinegar and season with salt and pepper. Purée the mixture, preferably using an immersion blender, until you have a smooth and velvety mixture. Pass the mixture through a fine-mesh sieve, then cover and refrigerate until well chilled, at least 1 hour.

5. Ladle the chilled gazpacho into individual bowls. Add a drizzle each of garlic cream and olive oil, followed by a sprinkle of piment d'Espelette. Top with the croutons.

PLANTIA'S ONION SOUP

SERVES 6

It's hard to imagine a bigger French cliché than onion soup. It's right up there with the mustache-sporting, striped-top-wearing, baguette-carrying guy pedaling his bicycle. When he sits down in a bistro to have onion soup, he's probably whistling "La Vie en Rose." And let's not forget the beret! I actually quite like that guy—and I *love* onion soup. In fact, it's a mystery to me that I didn't include a recipe for it in *A Kitchen in France*, though now, like so many things in life, I know why. It made me so happy to discover, talking to the old-timers of St Yzans, that Plantia, the lady who ran the restaurant in our house years ago, cooked her onion soup just like I do. Monsieur Gilet told me that her secret was to include duck fat in the recipe. I have been doing that for years. He also told me that she wouldn't use just any cheese for the tartines, instead opting for something special and flavorful, like Comté or aged Gruyère—just like I do. I call this Plantia's soup, but it's also my soup. It turns out they are the same wonderful cliché.

¼ CUP / 60 G RENDERED DUCK FAT
OR BUTTER

2 POUNDS / 1 KG LARGE YELLOW
ONIONS, THINLY SLICED

2 QUARTS / 2 LITERS CHICKEN
STOCK

⅓ CUP / 80 ML DRY WHITE WINE

LEAVES FROM A FEW SPRIGS OF
FRESH THYME

FINE SEA SALT AND FRESHLY
GROUND BLACK PEPPER

6 THICK SLICES RUSTIC
COUNTRY BREAD

½ POUND / 230 G CHEESE,
PREFERABLY COMTÉ, THINLY SLICED

1 TABLESPOON SHERRY VINEGAR

1. In a large pot or Dutch oven, heat the duck fat over medium-low heat. Add the onions and cook, stirring often, until softened, about 15 minutes.

2. Preheat the oven to 400°F / 200°C.

3. Add the chicken stock, wine, and thyme and season with salt and pepper. Bring to a simmer and continue to cook for 15 minutes. The soup should have a nice velvety consistency.

4. Put the bread on a baking sheet and top each slice with cheese. Toast in the oven until the cheese has melted and is slightly golden, a few minutes.

5. Add the sherry vinegar to the soup and adjust the seasoning with salt and pepper as needed. Ladle the soup into bowls, add a cheese tartine on top of each, and sprinkle with salt and pepper.

LOBSTER BISQUE

As a little girl growing up in Hong Kong, I would often yearn for French food, to re-create memories of summers spent in France with my grandmother. I would sometimes manage to cajole my food-obsessed father into taking us to a nice French restaurant for Sunday lunch. I would order all the classics: escargots with butter and garlic, steak with mushroom and red wine sauce, crème brûlée. But nothing made me feel quite as grown up as delicious and fancy lobster bisque, served by a waiter in a white jacket, pouring it into my bowl from a shiny silver ladle. I don't like my bisque too thick or too liquidy, and it definitely must have bits of lobster in it. This is admittedly not a recipe I cook all the time—but, once in a while, when I'm in a posh mood, I decide to go for it, to make my little girls happy and also for that little girl from Hong Kong who never fell out of love with lobster bisque.

2¼ POUNDS / 1 KG LIVE LOBSTERS
(ABOUT 2 MEDIUM)

2 TABLESPOONS EXTRA-VIRGIN
OLIVE OIL

1 MEDIUM CARROT, PEELED AND
THINLY DICED

2 MEDIUM SHALLOTS, THINLY DICED

2 GARLIC CLOVES, MINCED

FINE SEA SALT AND FRESHLY
GROUND BLACK PEPPER

½ CUP / 120 ML COGNAC

¾ CUP / 180 ML DRY WHITE WINE

2 TABLESPOONS TOMATO PASTE

1 CUP / 150 G CANNED CRUSHED
TOMATOES

1 BOUQUET GARNI (RECIPE BELOW)

1 TABLESPOON HONEY

1 TEASPOON SAFFRON THREADS

3 TABLESPOONS / 45 G UNSALTED
BUTTER, AT ROOM TEMPERATURE

3 TABLESPOONS ALL-PURPOSE
FLOUR

¼ TEASPOON CAYENNE PEPPER

1 CUP / 250 ML HEAVY CREAM

PINCH OF PIMENT D'ESPELETTE OR
MILD CHILE POWDER

A FEW FRESH CHIVES, FINELY
CHOPPED

BOUQUET GARNI

A mixture of fresh herbs and bay leaf, a bouquet garni is wonderful for flavoring soups and stews. Tie together with kitchen twine: 3 sprigs parsley, 1 sprig sage, 1 sprig rosemary, 1 sprig thyme, and 1 bay leaf. Add the herb bundle to the dish when directed and discard before serving.

1. Put the lobsters in the freezer for 20 minutes.

2. Using a sharp chef's knife, cut each lobster in half lengthwise, reserving all the liquid, coral, and creamy parts in a bowl. Cut the claws and tail from the rest of the lobster. Chop the remaining parts, including the shells, into several pieces.

3. In a large pot, heat the olive oil over medium heat. Add the lobster claws, tails, and shells, the carrot, shallots, and garlic and cook, stirring occasionally, until the shells turn bright red, about 10 minutes. Season with salt and pepper.

4. Pour in the Cognac. Light a match and carefully ignite the cooking liquid to flambé the lobster shells, shaking the pot briskly until the flames die out. Pour in the white wine and simmer to reduce for 2 to 3 minutes. Add water to cover and bring to a gentle simmer.

5. Stir in the tomato paste, crushed tomatoes, bouquet garni, honey, and saffron threads. Simmer over medium-low heat for 30 minutes, or until the soup is very flavorful.

6. Strain the soup through a sieve into a large bowl. Remove the lobster claws and tails, let cool for 5 minutes, and then remove the meat from the shells. Chop the meat coarsely, reserve 2 tablespoons of it for garnish, and return the rest to the strained soup.

7. Pour the soup into the pot. Cover and continue to simmer for 20 minutes.

8. Meanwhile, make the coral butter. In a bowl, mix the softened butter and flour to make a paste. Whisk in the reserved lobster liquid, coral, and any creamy parts and season with salt and the cayenne.

9. Reduce the heat under the soup to as low as it will go. Scoop some of the bisque into the bowl with the butter mixture and whisk until thickened before gradually pouring the entire mixture into the pot, whisking constantly. Remove from the heat.

10. Pour in the cream. Purée the soup, preferably using an immersion blender. Adjust the seasoning. Reheat over very low heat. Do not boil.

11. Ladle the bisque into bowls, scatter the reserved lobster meat on top, and sprinkle with the piment d'Espelette and chives.

SIMPLE VEGETABLE POTAGE

~ SERVES 4 TO 6 ~

One of the many things I love about France is the quality of the produce, the abundance that is available at local markets. To me that is one of the corner-stones of the culture and what makes France, well, France. Coming home after a trip to town, baskets full of beautiful vegetables and fruits, makes me feel like a painter who has returned from the art store, armed with new brushes and a brand new color palette. All the vegetables are screaming "Pick me, pick me!" and you simply can't go wrong. Unless, of course, you buy far too much, and then you have to up your game if you're to do justice to it all.

The flip side of this situation, one that admittedly rarely occurs in my house, might happen in winter if we've neglected going to the market or if we've been away and haven't stocked up properly since. Then I get enormous pleasure from making a meal out of simple sturdy ingredients that I always have on hand but are never vying for my attention: a simple leek, some familiar carrots, the ever-present onions. This might not be a terribly exotic lineup, but somehow it always manages to do the job—even better when I can find a loaf of bread to toast and maybe some garlic to rub over it. This simple yet satisfying soup may be the best value meal I can possibly think of.

2 TABLESPOONS / 30 G UNSALTED BUTTER

1 POUND 5 OUNCES / 600 G MEDIUM CARROTS, PEELED AND DICED

2 RUSSET POTATOES, PEELED AND DICED

1 LARGE LEEK, FINELY CHOPPED

¼ TEASPOON GRATED NUTMEG

FINE SEA SALT AND FRESHLY GROUND BLACK PEPPER

1 QUART / 1 LITER CHICKEN OR VEGETABLE STOCK

⅔ CUP / 160 ML HEAVY CREAM, PLUS MORE FOR SERVING

1 TEASPOON TOMATO PASTE

A FEW FRESH CHIVES, FINELY CHOPPED

1. In a large pot, melt the butter over medium-low heat. Add the carrots, potatoes, and leek. Cook, stirring occasionally, until the vegetables are slightly tender, about 5 minutes.

2. Stir in the nutmeg and season with salt and pepper. Pour the stock into the pot and bring to a simmer. Cover, reduce the heat, and cook for 30 minutes.

3. Purée the soup, preferably using an immersion blender. Whisk together the cream and tomato paste until smooth and then blend into the soup.

4. Reheat over low heat before ladling the soup into bowls and serving each with a drizzle of cream, if desired, and a dash of chives.

CELERY ROOT VELOUTÉ

Along with Tomato Gazpacho (page 72), this soup is probably the starter we served most often in our little restaurant—which frankly came as a surprise. I wanted something that we could make in advance, something simple but luxurious. So one night I came up with this creamy soup with a little kiss of mustard and served it with a slice of crisp bacon. I was worried that people might be disappointed, find it too straightforward, but instead it became a hit. I don't think it's a soup you can have too much of, but it works especially well as an appetizer, familiar enough to be pleasant yet interesting enough to hint at what lies ahead. Oddur, our resident sommelier, always paired this soup with a local Sauvignon Blanc, which I think is perfect.

3 TABLESPOONS / 45 G SALTED BUTTER

1 CELERY ROOT (ABOUT 2 POUNDS / 900 G), PEELED AND CUT INTO SMALL CUBES

FINE SEA SALT AND FRESHLY GROUND BLACK PEPPER

2 CUPS / 500 ML WHOLE MILK

¾ CUP / 180 ML CHICKEN STOCK

1 TABLESPOON DIJON MUSTARD

EXTRA-VIRGIN OLIVE OIL

PIMENT D'ESPELETTE OR MILD CHILE POWDER

6 SLICES BACON, COOKED UNTIL CRISP

1. In a large pot, melt the butter over medium-low heat. Add the celery root, season with salt and pepper, and cook for 5 minutes. Pour in the milk and stock and bring the soup to a simmer. Cover, reduce the heat, and simmer until the celery root is tender, about 20 minutes.

2. Purée the soup, preferably using an immersion blender. Stir in the mustard and season with salt and pepper as needed. Serve hot, drizzling each portion with a little olive oil and sprinkling with a pinch of piment d'Espelette. Top each bowl with a slice of bacon.

VICHYSSOISE

SERVES 4 TO 6

During my student days in Paris I'd make this soup practically every day because it was cheap, I liked it, and, frankly, I didn't know how to cook much else. My friend Isabelle's family has a house in Brittany and we'd go there on weekends for a little escape. Isa's mother (who is Swedish) would often make this soup, and on one visit I asked her to teach me how to make it. I guess I never stopped, and having it still reminds me of my younger days. I like to say that this soup can be served hot or cold, which is true, but in reality I prefer it hot with a loaf of country bread and a glass of good red wine.

2 TABLESPOONS / 30 G SALTED BUTTER

8 LARGE LEEKS, LIGHT AND DARK GREEN PARTS ONLY, TRIMMED, FINELY CHOPPED, AND WELL RINSED

3 LARGE RUSSET POTATOES, PEELED AND DICED

2 TABLESPOONS ALL-PURPOSE FLOUR

PINCH OF GRATED NUTMEG

1 QUART / 1 LITER CHICKEN OR VEGETABLE STOCK

1 CUP / 250 ML HEAVY CREAM

FINE SEA SALT AND FRESHLY GROUND BLACK PEPPER

A FEW FRESH CHIVES, FINELY CHOPPED

1. In a large pot, melt the butter over medium heat. Add the leeks and potatoes and sauté for 2 minutes. Sprinkle in the flour and nutmeg, stir to incorporate, and then pour in the stock. Bring to a simmer, then cover, reduce the heat to low, and cook for 30 minutes.

2. Pour in the cream and season with salt and pepper. Purée the soup, preferably using an immersion blender. You can serve this soup hot or cold, depending on your taste. Sprinkle with a dash of chopped chives before serving.

PLANTIA'S SPRING VEGETABLE STEW

Let me tell you about Il Professore! He was a man I met years ago during lunchtime at a restaurant in Rome, probably on our honeymoon. Oddur and I were having a simple pasta dish with a glass of wine when the plump, bespectacled man sitting at the table next to us leaned over. "You should try some of this," he said and handed over a platter jammed with rice-filled tomatoes. We liked the tomatoes, and so Il Professore introduced himself and continued: "There is another thing you must try." He summoned the waiter, who soon brought another platter, this one filled with the most luscious green vegetables. This was my first brush with *vignarola*, a classic vegetable stew made from all the greenest offerings of spring. Since then I've made versions of *vignarola* every year, summoning my army of little hands to help out with the shelling and peeling.

When I moved to St Yzans, I started asking around for old recipes from Plantia and was told that her absolute favorite thing to cook was fava beans, and that a spring vegetable stew was her signature dish. Monsieur Teyssier remembered that she had drafted all the boys in the village to find her fava beans wherever they could. He had the pleasure of tasting the stew cooked by Plantia's granddaughter, Jacqueline, and so he helped me piece together this recipe, which I hope does justice to Plantia's version. In any case I'm sure she is happy to have the smell of fresh fava beans and artichokes once more perfuming the kitchens at No 1 rue de Loudenne.

2 LARGE ARTICHOKES OR
4 OR 5 SMALL ARTICHOKES

1 LEMON, HALVED

2 TABLESPOONS EXTRA-VIRGIN
OLIVE OIL

2 OUNCES / 50 G PANCETTA OR
GUANCIALE, CHOPPED

2 TO 3 SPRING ONIONS, WHITE AND
GREEN PARTS, THINLY SLICED

FINE SEA SALT AND FRESHLY
GROUND BLACK PEPPER

2 CUPS / 250 TO 300 G FRESH
OR FROZEN SHELLED LARGE FAVA
BEANS, PEELED

2 CUPS / 250 TO 300 G FRESH OR
FROZEN GREEN PEAS

½ SMALL HEAD ROMAINE LETTUCE,
FINELY CHOPPED

SMALL HANDFUL OF FRESH
FLAT-LEAF PARSLEY LEAVES,
CHOPPED

SMALL HANDFUL OF FRESH MINT
LEAVES, CHOPPED

1. *If you have large artichokes:* Using a sharp knife, cut off each artichoke stem until flush with the bottom. Working your way around the artichoke, trim off leaves until the pale leaves appear. Cut off the dark, prickly top of the artichoke until you have only pale color left. You may need to cut off quite a bit. Next, cut each artichoke in half from top to bottom. With a small spoon, remove the prickly spines and fuzzy choke. Cut each half into 4 wedges. As you work, rub the artichokes with half of the lemon to keep them from browning. (Reserve the other lemon half for later.)

2. *If you have small artichokes:* Same as above, but you won't need to trim away quite as much (you can leave a little of the stem). Simply cut the artichokes in half, and you don't have to remove any fuzzy choke.

3. In a medium pot or shallow saucepan, heat the olive oil over medium heat. Add the pancetta and spring onions and cook until the onions soften, 2 to 3 minutes. Add the artichokes and season with salt and pepper. Add a couple tablespoons water, cover, and cook over low heat for 10 minutes.

4. Add the fava beans, peas, and romaine and season with salt and pepper. Add a tablespoon or two of water if the pan seems dry. Cover again and cook until all of the vegetables are tender, about 15 minutes.

5. Just before serving, drizzle with 1 teaspoon lemon juice and sprinkle with the parsley and mint.

CHESTNUT AND POTATO GALETTES

SERVES 10 TO 12

If you have already glanced at all the recipes in this book, and if you are perceptive, you may have noticed two things: my love for pancakes and my even stronger love for everything chestnut. Of course, I try to disguise my weakness for pancakes by calling them different names, like galettes, crêpes, etc. But the fact remains that I do love a pancake meal, especially if there's a twist, and especially if that twist is chestnuts, which lend a meaty quality to this vegetarian dish. Top these with a poached egg and this is exactly the type of dish I'd be happy to have for lunch at a bistro in Paris. I like to pair the galettes with a well-chosen white Burgundy, preferably an older one.

1 POUND / 450 G RUSSET POTATOES

8 OUNCES / 230 G PEELED COOKED CHESTNUTS (BOTTLED OR VACUUM-PACKED)

½ CUP / 60 G ALL-PURPOSE FLOUR

1 TEASPOON BAKING POWDER

¼ TEASPOON GRATED NUTMEG

½ CUP / 120 ML HEAVY CREAM

⅓ CUP / 80 ML WHOLE MILK

2 LARGE EGGS, BEATEN

FINE SEA SALT AND FRESHLY GROUND BLACK PEPPER

EXTRA-VIRGIN OLIVE OIL

1. Preheat the oven to 250°F / 120°C. Line a baking sheet with parchment paper.

2. Peel and wash the potatoes and cut them into ½-inch / 1.3 cm cubes. Put them in a saucepan, cover them with salted water, and boil until tender, about 15 minutes. Drain well and then mash with a potato masher. Separately, mash the cooked chestnuts with a fork; it's okay if they aren't perfectly smooth.

3. Put the potatoes in a large bowl and add the flour, baking powder, nutmeg, heavy cream, milk, and eggs. Mix with a wooden spoon until you get a smooth dough. Season with salt and pepper and then fold in the chestnuts.

4. In small nonstick skillet, heat a little olive oil over medium-high heat. Once it's hot, pour in a small ladle of batter, just enough to coat the bottom of the pan, and cook until golden brown on each side, flipping once, about 3 minutes per side. Put it on the lined baking sheet and transfer to the oven to keep warm while you repeat with the remaining batter to make about two dozen galettes. Serve warm.

OYSTERS AND PORCINI:
THE ESSENCE OF MÉDOC

WHEN YOU HAVE LIVED IN CITIES ALL YOUR LIFE you get used to the idea of oysters and wild mushrooms as luxuries. Waiters at your favorite restaurants will lean in and whisper in your ear that they have in their possession a number of fresh porcini, but not *that* many, so you should probably order fast. An expensive oyster platter ordered automatically calls for a bottle of Champagne.

Then you move to Médoc and before you know it you are finding more porcini every day than you can possibly eat and oysters are practically a dime a dozen. You spend Saturdays with friends at local oyster huts eating more oysters than you should and drinking wine that restaurants in Paris would use only for cooking. And you have more fun.

As a tribute to our region and to everybody's palate we served oysters all the time in our restaurant at No 1 rue de Loudenne. Almost every night, someone, often Miles (or Messy Miles as we called him when he opened the oysters), had to shuck a few dozen oysters. We'd serve them as an unexpected appetizer—with Champagne if we were quick; if we were slow, with the white wine.

My biggest regret about this past summer has to do with the porcini.

When we decided to open the restaurant, I had this dream that toward the end of its run, maybe even on closing night, we'd have a big porcini feast. The last evening was scheduled for early September, not really porcini season yet—so a very impractical fantasy, I know. But I dreamed that we'd summon the team for a porcini hunt that would yield an enormous amount of the most delicious, beautiful specimens. Then we'd brush off most of the dirt and display them in various places in the dining rooms, most prominently as a centerpiece on the big table in the harvest room, where we'd fill a platter with a mountain of porcini. We'd inundate the table with oysters and Champagne, and when it was time to take orders, we'd break open a big old Grand Cru and I'd select a few porcini from the middle of the table, slice them finely tableside, season them with olive oil, salt, and pepper, and everybody would indulge. The menu to follow that night would be saturated with porcini and everybody would leave happy.

This evening didn't happen. Not yet. But one day it will.

CHANTERELLE AND GARLIC TARTLETS

~ SERVES 6 ~

They say that real Médocains like to talk about only a limited number of subjects: wine, *bien sûr,* hunting, oysters, and mushrooms. And of these topics, everybody's favorite is mushrooms. Because they are foraged rather than grown, they are shrouded in mystery. People have their favorite spots, their secret spots. Soon after I moved to Médoc I got the hang of finding porcini mushrooms, which appear in late September or early October. But then I realized that mushroom mania actually starts earlier, in late summer, when the conditions are right for golden chanterelles. They are delicious panfried in butter with the classic combination of parsley and garlic. I love taking them a step further and adding them to a tartlet, with crème fraîche forming a luscious bed for the mushrooms. For the tartlet dough, I use a recipe that's taken me years to develop. I've tried and tested so many versions and for me this is the one that works best.

FOR THE SAVORY TART DOUGH

2 CUPS / 240 G ALL-PURPOSE FLOUR, PLUS MORE FOR ROLLING

½ TEASPOON FINE SEA SALT

9 TABLESPOONS / 125 G COLD UNSALTED BUTTER, CUT INTO CUBES

1 LARGE EGG

3 TABLESPOONS ICE-COLD WATER

1. Preheat the oven to 350°F / 180°C. Arrange six 4-inch / 10 cm tartlet pans on a baking sheet.

2. **MAKE THE TART DOUGH.** In a large bowl, whisk together the flour and salt. Add the butter and work it into the flour with your fingers until the mixture is crumbly. Make a well in the center and add the egg and water. Mix with your hands until the dough comes together and forms a ball. Wrap in plastic wrap and refrigerate for at least 1 hour, or overnight.

3. On a lightly floured surface, roll out the dough to a ⅛-inch / 3 mm thickness. Cut 6 rounds of dough at least 1 inch / 2.5 cm larger than the tartlet pans. Line the pans with the dough rounds, cutting off any excess. Prick the dough with a fork.

4. **MAKE THE FILLING.** In a bowl, whisk together the crème fraîche, egg yolk, half of the garlic, and the nutmeg. Season with salt and pepper.

5. Divide the mixture among the tartlet pans. Transfer the baking sheet to the oven and bake until golden brown, about 8 minutes.

FOR THE FILLING

5 TABLESPOONS / 75 ML CRÈME
FRAÎCHE

1 LARGE EGG YOLK

2 GARLIC CLOVES, MINCED

PINCH OF GRATED NUTMEG

FINE SEA SALT AND FRESHLY
GROUND BLACK PEPPER

1 TABLESPOON / 15 G UNSALTED
BUTTER

½ POUND / 230 G CHANTERELLE
MUSHROOMS

CHOPPED FRESH FLAT-LEAF
PARSLEY LEAVES

6. Meanwhile, in a large sauté pan, heat the butter over medium-high heat. When it is hot, add the mushrooms and remaining garlic, season with salt and pepper, and cook, stirring just once or twice, until the mushrooms are golden, about 3 minutes.

7. Spoon the mushrooms on top of the tartlets. Return to the oven to bake until the pastry is golden, about 10 minutes longer.

8. Sprinkle with parsley and serve immediately.

POTATO CROQUETTES WITH BAYONNE HAM

SERVES 6

Here is a typical scene from my kitchen on any given night: I'm peeling potatoes and frankly in a hurry to tend to other, more rewarding parts of the cooking. So I ask whoever is next to me, my husband, the children, or even a guest, "Don't you think that's enough potatoes?" The answer is almost always the same: silence, then a hesitant, "Well, I think we could do with a few more." Because I have a deep-seated fear of cooking too little food, I always listen and then we end up with a small mountain of mashed potatoes that we simply can't finish. The good thing is that they are easily reinvented the following day, such as in these little croquettes. Frying them in oil gives them a thin crisp exterior, and the Bayonne ham adds delicious flavor. These croquettes go equally well with cold beer or yesterday's wine, whatever that happened to be.

1 POUND / 450 G RUSSET POTATOES

1 CUP / 90 G GRATED CHEESE, SUCH AS GRUYÈRE OR COMTÉ

2 TABLESPOONS / 30 G UNSALTED BUTTER

1 TABLESPOON CRÈME FRAÎCHE

¼ TEASPOON GRATED NUTMEG

6 SLICES BAYONNE HAM OR PROSCIUTTO, CHOPPED

1 LARGE EGG

½ CUP / 60 G ALL-PURPOSE FLOUR

½ CUP / 75 G PANKO OR UNSEASONED DRIED BREAD CRUMBS

¼ CUP / 60 ML VEGETABLE OIL

FINE SEA SALT AND FRESHLY GROUND BLACK PEPPER

CHOPPED FRESH FLAT-LEAF PARSLEY (OPTIONAL)

1. Peel the potatoes and cut them into ½-inch / 1.3 cm cubes. Put them in a saucepan, cover with salted water, and boil over medium-high heat until tender, about 15 minutes. Drain well and then mash with a potato masher. Add the cheese, butter, crème fraîche, nutmeg, and ham.

2. In a small bowl, beat the egg. Put the flour in a second bowl and the bread crumbs in a third. Shape the potato mixture into small balls, each about the size of a walnut (you should get 10 to 12). Dust with flour, dip in the egg to coat, and then roll in the bread crumbs.

3. In a large skillet, heat the oil over high heat. You can test if it's ready by throwing in a small piece of bread; if the bread turns golden in a few seconds the oil is ready. Fry the croquettes on both sides until golden brown, about 1 minute per side. Drain on paper towels.

4. Season the hot croquettes with salt and pepper and sprinkle with parsley, if you like, before serving.

PEARL ONION TARTES TATIN

~ SERVES 8 ~

If my kitchen were a stage and my cooking a musical, then the chorus would be tartlets—never really the star but somehow the catchiest part of the play. During our restaurant days and nights, I think we had some sort of tartlet on the menu every single time. The sheer abundance of kale in our vegetable garden meant that often we had kale tartlets with sour cream and bacon. When we could get our hands on chanterelles, they'd replace the kale. But when we tired of kale, and when there were no mushrooms, we made this third version, which requires a little more work but more than makes up for the effort with pure tastiness. While caramelized onions and puff pastry are delicious as a pair, syrupy balsamic vinegar provides the magic finishing touch.

1 POUND 2 OUNCES / 500 G PEARL ONIONS

8 OUNCES / 230 G FROZEN PUFF PASTRY, THAWED

⅔ CUP / 70 G CONFECTIONERS' SUGAR

8 TEASPOONS / 40 G UNSALTED BUTTER

BALSAMIC VINEGAR, FOR SERVING

1. Preheat the oven to 400°F / 200°C.

2. In a large pot of boiling water, blanch the pearl onions for 5 minutes to loosen their skins and partially cook them. Drain and set aside to cool. Peel the onions.

3. Roll out the puff pastry as thinly as possible and cut out 8 rounds (large enough to fit into 4-inch / 10 cm tartlet pans). Set the pastry rounds aside.

4. Generously sprinkle confectioners' sugar into each of 8 empty tartlet pans until you can't see the base of the pan and put a teaspoon of butter in the center. Press gently with your finger so the butter is slightly spread. Spoon the pearl onions on top in an even layer.

5. Top the onions with the puff pastry, tucking the edges around the onions and into the mold. Using the palm of your hand, flatten the dough so you can see nice little onion bumps.

6. Put the tartlets on a baking sheet and bake them until golden brown and bubbling, 12 to 15 minutes.

7. Invert the tartlets onto plates and serve hot with a drizzle of balsamic vinegar.

POTATO AND CHARD GALETTES

SERVES 4 TO 6

We are a family that favors three-course meals. We all like to sit down to lunch or dinner, eat, and share stories; often the meal is the main event of the day Once in a while we break tradition and have a snack meal, which our boy Hudson loves. Then I make all sorts of salads; we have cold cuts, cold fish, and often serve everything in the most casual way, sometimes even standing up in the kitchen, often with loud music in the background—party meals, I guess you could call them. I am really fond of traditional Jewish brunches, complete with bagels and smoked fish, and this affinity often finds its way into my buffet lunches. These galettes, studded with Swiss chard and showered with lemon zest and fresh herbs, are my version of potato latkes. They are fun to make and so delicious with smoked salmon or trout on the side and a crisp cold beer.

4 LARGE EGG YOLKS

4 MEDIUM RUSSET POTATOES, PEELED AND COARSELY GRATED

1 MEDIUM YELLOW ONION, FINELY CHOPPED

1 LARGE SWISS CHARD LEAF, FINELY CHOPPED

2 TABLESPOONS CHOPPED FRESH FLAT-LEAF PARSLEY LEAVES

1 CUP / 120 G ALL-PURPOSE FLOUR

PINCH OF GRATED NUTMEG

FINE SEA SALT AND FRESHLY GROUND BLACK PEPPER

VEGETABLE OIL, FOR FRYING

CRÈME FRAÎCHE, FOR SERVING

PINCH OF PIMENT D'ESPELETTE OR MILD CHILE POWDER

GRATED ZEST OF 1 LEMON

A SMALL HANDFUL OF CHOPPED FRESH HERBS, SUCH AS PARSLEY, MINT, OR DILL

1. In a large bowl, whisk the egg yolks. Put the grated potatoes in a clean kitchen towel and squeeze out excess water with your hands. Using a wooden spoon, mix in the potatoes, onion, Swiss chard, parsley, flour, and nutmeg. Season with salt and pepper.

2. Pour about 1¼ inches / 3 cm oil into a large sauté pan and heat over high heat. You can test if it's hot enough by throwing in a small piece of bread; if the bread turns golden in a few seconds, the oil is ready.

3. Meanwhile, form the potato mixture into small, slightly rounded patties about 3 inches / 7.5 cm across. You should have about 10. Fry them in the hot oil until golden brown on both sides, about 2 minutes per side. Drain on paper towels.

4. Serve warm, each topped with a dollop of crème fraîche and a sprinkling of piment d'Espelette, lemon zest, and fresh herbs.

PUMPKIN QUICHE WITH BACON

~ SERVES 6 ~

One of my favorite ways to prepare pumpkins is to roast them with oil and herbs and serve them as a side dish, often with pork or beef. I like this way of cooking them so much that I wondered if maybe I didn't really need the meat; maybe I could just serve them on their own, like that, for lunch or as a starter. It turns out that the squash still needed a little something—so gradually this recipe emerged, where the roasted pumpkin is incorporated into a quiche.

1¼ POUNDS / 600 G PUMPKIN OR OTHER WINTER SQUASH

2 TABLESPOONS EXTRA-VIRGIN OLIVE OIL, PLUS MORE FOR DRIZZLING

LEAVES FROM 1 SPRIG OF FRESH ROSEMARY

FINE SEA SALT AND FRESHLY GROUND BLACK PEPPER

3½ OUNCES / 100 G BACON, CUT INTO LARDONS OR DICED

1 LARGE YELLOW ONION, THINLY SLICED

2 LARGE EGG YOLKS

1 CUP / 250 ML HEAVY CREAM

¼ TEASPOON GRATED NUTMEG

2 LARGE EGG WHITES

8 OUNCES / 230 G FROZEN PUFF PASTRY, THAWED

1. Preheat the oven to 400°F / 200°C.

2. Cut the pumpkin in half and scoop out the seeds. Slice the pumpkin into 6-inch / 15 cm wedges. Line a roasting pan with parchment paper and lay out the pumpkin wedges on top. Drizzle with olive oil and season with the rosemary and salt and pepper. Roast, turning them over once, until golden and tender, about 30 minutes.

3. Meanwhile, in a large sauté pan, heat 2 tablespoons olive oil over medium-high heat. Add the bacon and cook until browned, about 3 minutes. Reduce the heat to low, add the onion, and season with salt and pepper. Cook, stirring occasionally, until the onion is tender and slightly golden brown, about 18 minutes.

4. Discard the pumpkin skin and purée the flesh in a food processor or mash well in a bowl with a fork. Set aside in a bowl to cool.

5. Stir the egg yolks, cream, and nutmeg into the pumpkin. Season with salt and pepper. Add the onion/bacon mixture, discarding excess oil.

6. Using an electric mixer, beat the egg whites to stiff peaks. Fold the whites into the pumpkin mixture.

7. On a lightly floured surface, roll out the dough to a ⅛-inch / 3 mm thickness. Line a 10-inch / 25 cm tart pan with the puff pastry, trimming excess from the edges, and prick the bottom several times with a fork.

8. Scoop the pumpkin mixture into the tart shell. Bake until the pastry is crisp and golden and the filling is set, about 35 minutes. Let cool for 5 minutes before serving.

PUFF PASTRY SHELLS WITH LANGOUSTINES AND SCALLOPS

~ SERVES 4 ~

I love a good vol-au-vent, or in this case *bouchée à la Reine*: delicious puff pastry, stuffed with a creamy filling and topped with a chic little hat. In fact, one of my first blog posts was of a recipe for *bouchée à la Reine* with a mushroom and chicken filling, and it remains, to this day, the most re-blogged, tagged, and pinned image of any on the blog. It was one of my earliest posts, and, if I am being honest, I know I can do better. This version, with langoustines and scallops, is my absolute favorite: extra luxurious, filled with seafood, and perfect to be enjoyed in the company of those who feel as strongly about *bouchée à la Reine* as I do.

1 TABLESPOON EXTRA-VIRGIN OLIVE OIL

12 MEDIUM WHITE MUSHROOMS, SLICED

1 MEDIUM LEEK, WHITE PART ONLY, THINLY SLICED

FINE SEA SALT AND FRESHLY GROUND BLACK PEPPER

¼ CUP / 60 ML DRY WHITE WINE

¾ CUP / 180 ML CHICKEN STOCK

8 LANGOUSTINES OR MEATY CRAWFISH TAILS, SHELLED

4 LARGE SEA SCALLOPS, HALVED HORIZONTALLY

5 TABLESPOONS / 75 ML CRÈME FRAÎCHE

4 BAKED PUFF PASTRY SHELLS (4½ INCH / 11.5 CM DIAMETER)

LEAVES FROM A FEW SPRIGS OF FRESH TARRAGON, CHOPPED

1. Preheat the oven to 325°F / 160°C.

2. In a large sauté pan, heat the olive oil over medium heat. Add the mushrooms and leek, season with salt and pepper, and cook until softened, a few minutes. Pour in the wine and simmer for 2 minutes to reduce. Add the chicken stock, bring to a boil, and cook for 8 minutes.

3. Add the langoustines and scallops, season with salt and pepper, and cook until just cooked through, about 3 minutes. Reduce the heat and stir in the crème fraîche. Remove the filling from the heat and season with salt and pepper.

4. Put the pastry shells and tops ("hats") on a baking sheet and heat in the oven until hot, 5 to 8 minutes.

5. Spoon the filling into the shells, sprinkle with the tarragon, and place the pastry "hat" on top. Serve immediately.

BUTTERNUT PANCAKES
WITH SAGE BROWN BUTTER

We don't grow our own yet, but in autumn we tend to build up a small collection of pumpkins and squash in various shapes and sizes. We decorate our tables with them, and for a few weeks it seems we are drowning in pumpkins. Then, as the season progresses, we start cutting them up one by one; many end up in soups, while others get roasted as a side dish. The really lucky ones end up in delicious little creations like these pancakes that are so simple to make, yet feel quite decadent and "grown up" when drenched in sage and butter sauce. The words "light" and "rich" seem contradictory, but they are the ones I would pick to describe these pancakes.

1⅓ CUPS / 200 G BUTTERNUT SQUASH PURÉE (SEE NOTE)

1 LARGE EGG

⅓ CUP / 80 ML CRÈME FRAÎCHE

⅓ CUP / 30 G FRESHLY GRATED PARMESAN CHEESE (OPTIONAL)

1½ CUPS / 180 G ALL-PURPOSE FLOUR

1 TEASPOON BAKING POWDER

FINE SEA SALT

5½ TABLESPOONS / 80 G UNSALTED BUTTER, PLUS MORE FOR THE SKILLET

A SMALL BUNCH OF FRESH SAGE LEAVES

note
To make the purée, peel, seed, and cube about half a medium butternut squash, then roast it in a preheated 350°F / 180°C oven until very tender, about 20 minutes. Purée using a potato ricer or food processor, or mash by hand.

1. In a bowl, mix the butternut purée, egg, and crème fraîche. Using a wooden spoon, stir in the Parmesan (if using), flour, baking powder, and a pinch of salt until you get a smooth batter.

2. Lightly butter a large cast-iron skillet or sauté pan and set over medium heat. Using about half of the batter, drop 4 or 5 pancakes into the pan. Let them cook until the bubbles on the surface start to pop and the undersides are golden brown, about 1 minute, then flip them over. Cook just to set the other side, about 1 minute. Repeat with the remaining batter.

3. In a small saucepan, heat the 5½ tablespoons / 80 g butter over medium heat. Add a pinch of salt and the sage leaves and cook until the butter turns golden brown and the sage leaves are crisp, a few minutes.

4. Serve the pancakes with a drizzle of the browned butter and sage leaves on top.

WHITE ASPARAGUS SOUFFLÉ

⟿ SERVES 6 ⟽

You can't write a French cookbook without including at least one soufflé—in fact, there is probably a law against it. A corollary is that you can't really come to France without having at least one . . . which is probably why I get so many requests for a soufflé during the cooking workshops I host in my kitchen here in Médoc. Sometimes we make a sweet one, with berries, or a classic chocolate one. More often than not we turn lunch into an elegant affair with a swanky cheese soufflé. In spring and during large parts of the summer, artichokes find their way into our soufflés, which is wonderful, but for a precious few weeks in April and May we make the most special soufflé of all—the white whale of soufflés—with white asparagus. When you buy asparagus at the market, it's tempting to go for the pretty medium-size ones, perfectly bundled up, almost like a bouquet of flowers. But for a soufflé or a soup my advice is to go for the thick, huge, unshapely ones, which are more flavorful.

1 POUND / 450 G WHITE ASPARAGUS

5½ TABLESPOONS / 80 G UNSALTED BUTTER, PLUS MORE FOR THE RAMEKINS

⅔ CUP / 80 G ALL-PURPOSE FLOUR, PLUS MORE FOR THE RAMEKINS

2 CUPS / 500 ML WHOLE MILK

5 OUNCES / 150 G GRUYÈRE OR COMTÉ CHEESE, GRATED (ABOUT 1⅓ CUPS)

FINE SEA SALT AND FRESHLY GROUND BLACK PEPPER

4 LARGE EGG WHITES

4 LARGE EGG YOLKS

1. Cook the asparagus in boiling salted water until very tender, about 10 minutes. Drain and squeeze out any excess water with your hands. Purée in a food processor until smooth.

2. Butter and flour 6 (7-ounce / 210 ml) ramekins. Put them in the freezer for at least 15 minutes before filling them.

3. Preheat the oven to 400°F / 200°C.

4. In a medium saucepan, melt the 5½ tablespoons / 80 g butter over low heat. Whisk in the ⅔ cup / 80 g flour all at once and cook, still whisking, until combined, about 30 seconds. Slowly add the milk, whisking constantly. Add the puréed asparagus and cook, stirring, until thickened and the mixture coats the back of a spoon, 5 to 8 minutes. Add the cheese, stir until it melts, and then season with salt and pepper. Set aside to cool slightly.

5. Using an electric mixer, whip the egg whites to stiff peaks. Stir the yolks into the asparagus mixture. Using a rubber spatula, gently fold in the egg whites.

6. Pour the mixture into the ramekins, filling them three-quarters full. Put the ramekins on a baking sheet and bake until the soufflés are golden and well risen, about 15 minutes. Serve immediately.

WILD MUSHROOMS WITH AN EGG YOLK

SERVES 1

Mushrooms are a funny thing. It's hard to imagine a humbler food; they pop up seemingly overnight in dark, wet corners of the forest. Yet somehow they are a luxurious, sought-after delicacy: People go to extreme lengths to get their hands on them, searching for hours in the woods or forking out vast sums at the market. Eggs are equally humble but completely different. You can get them everywhere, all the time. What these two foods have in common is versatility. They enjoy a good relationship in various dishes, and when they fall in love and marry we call it a mushroom omelette. But what about taking a step back, just letting them flirt without shacking up? Here these two humble comfort foods dance playfully and seductively together.

A HANDFUL EACH OF PORCINI AND
CHANTERELLE MUSHROOMS

FINE SEA SALT AND FRESHLY
GROUND BLACK PEPPER

A KNOB OF BUTTER

1 LARGE EGG YOLK, PREFERABLY
ORGANIC

LEAVES FROM 1 SPRIG OF FRESH
FLAT-LEAF PARSLEY, CHOPPED

1. Slice the porcini ¼ inch / 6 mm thick.

2. Heat a sauté pan over medium-high heat until very hot. Add the mushrooms and season with salt and pepper. Cook until golden, 1 to 2 minutes per side, then add the butter.

3. Transfer to a plate, spoon the egg yolk in the center, and sprinkle with the parsley. Serve immediately.

SPRING FLAN WITH ZUCCHINI AND MINT

~ SERVES 8 TO 10 ~

Have you ever tried to keep up with a zucchini garden that has completely let loose and no matter how many salads, pastas, and ratatouilles you cook, you hardly make a dent in your green stockpile? For a few weeks this past summer it seemed to me that every time I glanced out the window overlooking the road that leads to our vegetable garden, some family member would be carrying home a crate filled with zucchini. So we stuffed them, used them in omelettes, fried them simply, Italian style. Still the mountain grew, and my zucchini appetite did the opposite.

Then I remembered a little dish I used to have at the most delightful tearoom in Paris, called Les Deux Abeilles, close to my old apartment. Run by a mother and daughter, it would always have a sophisticated, light, and flavorful flan or quiche that was right up my alley—and just what I needed to address the zucchini situation. If any dish in this book is ideal for "ladies who lunch," this is it, especially when served with a glass of crisp rosé.

2 TABLESPOONS EXTRA-VIRGIN OLIVE OIL, PLUS MORE FOR THE MUFFIN TIN

2 LARGE ZUCCHINI, HALVED LENGTHWISE, THEN SLICED CROSSWISE INTO THIN HALF-MOONS

2 MEDIUM SHALLOTS, FINELY CHOPPED

2 GARLIC CLOVES, THINLY SLICED

FINE SEA SALT AND FRESHLY GROUND BLACK PEPPER

5 LARGE EGGS

¼ CUP / 30 G CORNSTARCH

5 OUNCES / 150 G CHEESE, SUCH AS EMMENTAL OR GRUYÈRE, GRATED (ABOUT 1⅓ CUPS)

½ TEASPOON GRATED NUTMEG

2 TABLESPOONS FRESH LEMON JUICE

HANDFUL OF CHOPPED FRESH MINT, PLUS MORE FOR SERVING

1. Preheat the oven to 350°F / 180°C. Grease 10 cups of a standard muffin tin with olive oil.

2. In a large sauté pan, heat the 2 tablespoons olive oil over medium-high heat. Add the zucchini, shallots, and garlic. Season with salt and pepper and cook until slightly golden, a few minutes.

3. Meanwhile, in a large bowl, whisk together the eggs and cornstarch until smooth. Stir in the cheese and nutmeg and season with salt and pepper.

4. Remove the zucchini mixture from the heat and gently stir in the lemon juice and mint. Stir in the cheese mixture.

5. Divide the mixture among the 10 prepared muffin tin cups, filling them three-quarters full. Bake until slightly golden on top and the flans are set when you tap the edge of the pan, about 20 minutes.

6. Let sit for a few minutes before running a dull knife around the edges and unmolding. Top with mint and serve immediately.

BROILED OYSTERS WITH FOIE GRAS AND SAUTERNES

Wе live in oyster country. Every market we go to has an oysterman or two; every restaurant has oysters on the menu. On Sundays you can find oyster-men outside *boulangeries*, on street corners, outside (and even inside) supermarkets. In other words, where we live, oysters are not a rarity. Most of the oysters we get are local, from Oléron in the north or Cap Ferret in the south, but we even get oysters from Brittany.

We often served raw oysters in our pop-up restaurant, as a natural amuse-bouche, after the radishes with butter and some charcuterie. Once in a while, on a special night, we offered these instead, and I loved to see and hear people's reaction. Most of them said something like "I've never had oysters like this before" and usually followed that with "and I love them!"

12 OYSTERS IN THE SHELL

5 OUNCES / 150 G FOIE GRAS

¼ CUP / 60 ML SAUTERNES

COARSE SEA SALT AND FRESHLY
GROUND BLACK PEPPER

1. Preheat the broiler to high.

2. Shuck the oysters. Pour their liquid into a bowl (otherwise you won't have space for the Sauternes) and reserve for another use or discard. Reserve the oysters in their bottom shells; discard the top shells.

3. Slice the foie gras into 12 thin pieces and arrange one on top of each oyster. Divide the Sauternes among the oyster shells. Season with salt and pepper.

4. Sprinkle coarse salt on a small rimmed baking sheet to help steady the oysters and prevent them from toppling; place the oysters on top. Transfer to the broiler. Cook until the foie gras has melted slightly, 3 to 5 minutes. Serve immediately.

CHICKEN AND LEMON PÂTÉ EN CROÛTE

MAKES 1 TERRINE (11 × 4 INCH / 28 CM × 10 CM)

I guess it goes without saying that all the food in this book is "my kind of food"—
otherwise it wouldn't be in here. This recipe in particular, though, is really, and
I mean *really, my kind of food*. You can buy a very good *pâté en croûte* at the *épicerie*, but it
can never quite compare to the sheer joy and pride you get from a homemade one,
patiently crafted and vigorously enjoyed. This is a light, citrusy take on a classic *pâté
en croûte*, which is often made with foie gras or all pork.

1 POUND / 450 G BONELESS,
SKINLESS CHICKEN BREAST HALVES
(ABOUT 2)

4 TABLESPOONS MADEIRA

9 OUNCES / 250 G PORK SAUSAGE,
CASINGS REMOVED

9 OUNCES / 250 G SLICED HAM,
DICED

½ CUP / 80 G UNSALTED
PISTACHIOS

1 LARGE EGG, LIGHTLY BEATEN

1 MEDIUM SHALLOT, MINCED

1 TABLESPOON DIJON MUSTARD

1 TABLESPOON GRATED LEMON ZEST

½ TABLESPOON FRESH THYME

FINE SEA SALT AND FRESHLY
GROUND BLACK PEPPER

1 POUND / 450 G FROZEN PUFF
PASTRY, THAWED

1 LARGE EGG YOLK

1. Preheat the oven to 350°F / 180°C.

2. Cut one of the chicken breasts into strips and marinate it in a small
bowl with 1 tablespoon of the Madeira. Dice the other chicken breast
into small cubes and mix in the sausage meat, ham, pistachios, egg,
shallot, mustard, lemon zest, thyme, and remaining 3 tablespoons
Madeira. Season with salt and pepper. Let marinate for 20 minutes.

3. Assuming your puff pastry comes in two sheets, cut one crosswise
into two equal pieces. Use the whole sheet and one of the halves to line
the bottom and sides of an 11 × 4-inch / 28 cm × 10 cm terrine. (If you
do not have one, a 9 × 5-inch / 23 × 12.5 cm loaf pan makes a decent
substitute.) Leave a little overhang on all sides.

4. Put half of the sausage mixture in the pan, smoothing the top, then
add the chicken strips. Top with the remaining sausage mixture.

5. Put the second half sheet of pastry on top and seal the edges with
the one lining the pan, trimming any excess dough. Cut scraps into the
shape of leaves, about 6. Arrange decoratively on top. Pierce a hole in
the center of the loaf to make a steam vent. Lightly beat the egg yolk with
a little water and brush over the top of the pastry.

6. Put the terrine on a rimmed baking sheet to catch any drips. Bake
until golden brown on top and cooked through, about 1 hour
15 minutes.

7. Remove from the oven and let cool in the pan completely before
refrigerating until cold, at least 2 hours or overnight. To serve, unmold
the pâté by tipping the mold gently on its side, then cut into slices.

ROAST BONE MARROW WITH HERBS

∼ SERVES 4 ∼

One of my weaknesses, and I have many when it comes to food, is old-fashioned recipes, bourgeois-style slow-cooked stews, but also, going even further back in history, medieval dishes. I am a big believer in using every part of the animal, especially when we're talking about slathering a slice of really good country bread with a thick coat of delicious melted marrow, or fat—pure indulgence. Of course, the fat and the bread need a little help to achieve glory, so I mix in a few herbs and spices and salt. This little dish is perfect for a quick snack with a glass of good wine, either red or white. I also love serving it as a starter at lunch, probably in winter when the next act would be something like a hearty bean soup, a rabbit stew, or even a grand cassoulet. Usually I ask my butcher to give me small pieces of bone so each guest gets his own and doesn't have to share.

8 VEAL MARROW BONES (4 INCHES / 10 CM EACH)

1 CUP / 150 G FRESH FLAT-LEAF PARSLEY LEAVES, COARSELY CHOPPED

LEAVES FROM 2 SPRIGS OF FRESH ROSEMARY, FINELY CHOPPED

2 SMALL SHALLOTS, THINLY SLICED

2 TABLESPOONS EXTRA-VIRGIN OLIVE OIL

GRATED ZEST OF 1 LEMON

1 TABLESPOON FRESH LEMON JUICE

COARSE SEA SALT AND FRESHLY GROUND BLACK PEPPER

SLICES OF RUSTIC COUNTRY BREAD, TOASTED

1. Preheat the oven to 450°F / 230°C.

2. Arrange the bones standing up, with their larger ends down, in a roasting pan. Roast the bones until the marrow is soft and golden, 15 to 20 minutes.

3. Meanwhile, prepare the salad. In a medium bowl, toss together the parsley, rosemary, shallots, olive oil, lemon zest, and lemon juice. Season with salt and pepper.

4. Put the marrow bones on plates, top with a sprinkling of coarse sea salt, and serve with the parsley salad and toast on the side and little spoons or knives for scooping out the marrow.

COUNTRY TERRINE

MAKES 1 TERRINE, SERVES 8 TO 10

I have vivid memories from my childhood summers in the southwest of France of old men carrying cheeses and various sausages in their handkerchiefs. They would buy a baguette, take out their pocketknives, and conjure up a feast at any time of the day, usually laid out on an old wine barrel or vegetable box. My fascination with "old men food" grew so strong that I asked my parents for a pocketknife for my birthday, an Opinel that I still have.

A staple of "old men food" is the rustic country terrine, and this particular recipe comes from Yves Lajoux, who is also known as "the forest whisperer." He lives not far from us here in Médoc, and he knows the land better than anyone. No one is better at finding wild mushrooms or strawberries and, according to him, no one makes a better terrine. I fell in love with this recipe some years ago and have made it regularly since, probably twice a year. It's an effort, but a fun one. You will need a meat grinder with a medium-hole plate, or you can ask your butcher to mince the chicken livers and pork meat for you.

5 OUNCES / 150 G CHICKEN LIVERS

1 POUND / 450 G COARSELY GROUND FATTY PORK SHOULDER

1 TEASPOON FINE SEA SALT

½ TEASPOON GROUND PINK PEPPERCORNS

½ TEASPOON FRESHLY GROUND BLACK PEPPER

¼ TEASPOON GRATED NUTMEG

¼ TEASPOON FRESHLY GROUND WHITE PEPPER

LEAVES FROM A SMALL BUNCH OF FRESH THYME (ABOUT 1 TEASPOON)

1 MEDIUM SHALLOT, THINLY SLICED

¼ CUP / 60 ML ARMAGNAC

2 TABLESPOONS PORT

1½ TABLESPOONS RED WINE VINEGAR

8 BAY LEAVES, PREFERABLY FRESH, IF AVAILABLE

1. In a large bowl, mix together all of the ingredients except for the bay leaves. Cover and refrigerate overnight.

2. The next day, preheat the oven to 400°F / 200°C.

3. Scoop the meat mixture into a 1½-quart / 1½ liter Dutch oven. Arrange the bay leaves decoratively on top and cover tightly with foil.

4. Put the Dutch oven in a large roasting pan and pour boiling water into the roasting pan so it comes nearly halfway up the sides of the Dutch oven to make a water bath. Cook in the oven for 45 minutes.

5. Reduce the oven temperature to 350°F / 180°C and cook for 20 minutes. Remove the foil and cook until the terrine registers 150° to 160°F / 65° to 71°C on a meat thermometer inserted into the center, another 25 to 40 minutes.

6. Remove from the water bath and let cool completely. Cover and refrigerate for at least 24 and up to 48 hours. Remove bay leaves before serving.

MAIN COURSES

POULET CHASSEUR *133*

CHICKEN MARENGO *134*

GUINEA HEN RAVIOLI *138*

ROAST DUCK *with* CHERRIES *142*

QUAIL STUFFED *with* FOIE GRAS *145*

QUAIL MILLEFEUILLE *146*

CASSOULET *150*

FOREST PIE *160*

BLACK PEPPERED FILETS MIGNONS
with COGNAC *161*

PORK TENDERLOIN *with* PRUNES
and RED WINE SAUCE *164*

BLACK PIG PORK CHOPS *166*

MONKFISH STEW *with* SAFFRON *169*

TURBOT *with* VIN JAUNE SAUCE *170*

SEA SCALLOPS *with* CAULIFLOWER PURÉE
and CAPERS *174*

CRAB FEUILLETÉ *176*

I SPENT LARGE portions of my childhood in various restaurants with my parents, their friends, my friends. I have countless memories of sitting at late-night banquet tables surrounded by members of the Hong Kong Lions Club, feasting on the finest delicacies, and having big lunches with my godfather, Uncle Fat Steven (that's what everyone calls him), watching him consume three whole chickens in the most delicate, precise manner. As I got older, it became my favorite pastime to find the best restaurants when I traveled.

When Oddur and I were romancing each other and he visited me in Paris, our main concern (well, aside from all the romance) was always where to have dinner. As an art director and an insufferable aesthete, to him the food has to be good but the place must look right as well. And by looking right I don't mean ornate or luxurious; it just has to have soul, a story. But to me the food is the most important.

As much as I hate to admit it, Oddur has a point: A restaurant is more than the sum of all its food. There is the decor and service, the music, the font on the menu, even the soap in the bathrooms. When we are both pleased, we know we've found someplace we'll return to again and again.

They say that the French invented the restaurant, and while just that would have been good enough, they went a step further and created different versions. There is the beloved bistro, an intimate spot, often very small, with tables almost on top of each other. The menu is usually ever-changing, representing what's fresh and in season (in the good ones, anyway). Then you have the noisy, boisterous brasseries, very often cavernous in size and serviced by an army of black-bow-tied waiters, whose starched white aprons touch the ground and who invariably can be found, several times a day, in the alleys outside these establishments smoking cigarettes. These are the places where you have huge plates of oysters and steaks (often mediocre) with piles of French fries. Above these two, looking down at them from lofty heights, is the older, more sophisticated brother, the *restaurant*. The restaurateur these days spends all his time dreaming of the Michelin stars that define his existence. He will do anything to achieve them.

We certainly weren't shooting for Michelin stars when we opened our little pop-up; and though our house is big, we did not plan on putting on bow ties. So a bistro it would be, an old-fashioned, country version. The food would reflect the season, and there would be an abundance of fruits and vegetables on display since nothing is as decorative and inviting as mountains of natural, colorful beauty. We never defined a formal concept, but if we had it might have been "granny goes to town," the country girl in her finest clothes, the tablecloth you use only on Sundays.

POULET CHASSEUR

This recipe is here as a result of an argument—not a serious one, so maybe it's better to call it a disagreement. My husband loves tomatoes the way I love chestnuts, and he tries to add them to everything. He adores the Italian version of hunter's chicken, with lots of red wine and tomato sauce, and kept asking me to make it. So I did. The problem, however, was that I don't really love that dish—so while he devoured it, I didn't eat that much. I kept telling him that French hunter's chicken, with mushrooms and white wine, is much better, and one day I cooked it unannounced. To make sure I'd get my point across I went to extra lengths, sourcing the finest farm chicken, picking the tarragon we were growing on our roof garden. His verdict: delicious, crispy, tasty, flavorful, "but I still love the tomato version." And I still disagree.

¾ CUP / 90 G ALL-PURPOSE FLOUR

FINE SEA SALT AND FRESHLY GROUND BLACK PEPPER

6 LARGE CHICKEN LEGS (THIGH AND DRUMSTICK)

5½ TABLESPOONS / 80 G UNSALTED BUTTER

6 TABLESPOONS / 90 ML EXTRA-VIRGIN OLIVE OIL

1 LARGE ONION, THINLY SLICED

2 SHALLOTS, THINLY SLICED

2 GARLIC CLOVES, THINLY SLICED

1 BOUQUET GARNI (SEE PAGE 79)

½ POUND / 230 G PORCINI MUSHROOMS, QUARTERED

3 TABLESPOONS COGNAC

¼ CUP / 60 ML WHITE WINE

¾ CUP / 180 ML CHICKEN STOCK

LEAVES FROM 1 BUNCH OF FRESH TARRAGON

1. Preheat the oven to 400°F / 200°C.

2. In a shallow baking dish, combine the flour, ½ teaspoon salt, and a pinch of pepper. Coat the chicken pieces with the mixture and shake off the excess.

3. Heat 4 tablespoons / 60 g of the butter and the oil in a large Dutch oven or other ovenproof pan over medium-high heat. Add the chicken and brown on all sides, 8 to 10 minutes. Transfer the pan to the oven and roast until the chicken is cooked through, 20 to 25 minutes.

4. Remove the chicken from the pan and keep warm on a platter. Put the pan with all its drippings over medium-high heat and add the onion, shallots, and garlic. Season with salt and pepper and cook until golden, about 4 minutes. Throw in the bouquet garni and mushrooms and continue to cook for 3 minutes.

5. Carefully add the Cognac, light a match, and ignite the Cognac. Once the flames die down, pour in the white wine and boil to reduce by three-quarters. Pour in the chicken stock and boil for 5 minutes.

6. Add the remaining 1½ tablespoons / 20 g butter and return the chicken to the pan. Reheat, spooning the sauce over the chicken. Scatter the tarragon all over. Season with salt and pepper as needed and serve immediately.

CHICKEN MARENGO

SERVES 4 TO 6

In our house we call this famous dish Napoleon's Chicken because it was originally cooked for him. He had just won a famous victory at the battle of Marengo and wanted to celebrate it with good food—good French food. The problem for his chef was that they were in Italy and all the familiar ingredients were hard to find. The chef put on his finest improvisational hat and whisked up a delicious chicken dish that pretended to be French but was probably more Italian than anything. Mr. Bonaparte loved the dish so much that he decided he would never eat anything else after any battle. Later this dish became fashionable in all the right Paris places, but, funnily enough, though the versions shared the name they never had the same ingredients. Chicken Marengo is less a recipe and more an idea that sends you off in the right direction; the details are up to you. So I experimented and came up with this version that has become much loved in our home. And I leave it to you to improve it.

1 WHOLE CHICKEN (5½ POUNDS /
2.5 KG), CUT INTO 6 TO 8 PIECES

FINE SEA SALT AND FRESHLY
GROUND BLACK PEPPER

2 TABLESPOONS ALL-PURPOSE
FLOUR

6 TABLESPOONS / 90 ML
EXTRA-VIRGIN OLIVE OIL

2 SHALLOTS, FINELY CHOPPED

1 MEDIUM CARROT, SLICED

6 GARLIC CLOVES, FINELY CHOPPED

1 BOUQUET GARNI (SEE PAGE 79)

¾ CUP / 200 ML DRY WHITE WINE

¼ CUP / 60 ML CHICKEN STOCK

1 CAN (14 OUNCES / 400 G) WHOLE
PEELED PLUM TOMATOES, DRAINED
AND COARSELY CHOPPED

2 TABLESPOONS TOMATO PASTE

12 FRESH LANGOUSTINES OR
CRAYFISH TAILS

⅓ CUP / 80 ML COGNAC

8 OUNCES / 200 G WHITE
MUSHROOMS, SLICED

LEAVES FROM 1 BUNCH OF FRESH
FLAT-LEAF PARSLEY, CHOPPED

1. Season the chicken pieces with salt and pepper and toss with the flour to coat. In a large Dutch oven, heat 3 tablespoons of the olive oil over medium-high heat. Add the chicken and brown on all sides until golden, 8 to 10 minutes.

2. Spoon off and discard any excess oil and then add the shallots, carrot, and 5 of the garlic cloves. Cook for 4 minutes over medium heat. Add the bouquet garni, season with salt and pepper, and add the white wine. Simmer to reduce for 2 minutes. Pour in the chicken stock and continue to simmer for 3 minutes.

3. Stir in the tomatoes and tomato paste and continue to cook for 3 minutes. Reduce the heat, season with salt and pepper, cover, and simmer until the chicken is cooked through, 35 to 45 minutes (larger pieces take more time to cook).

4. Meanwhile, in a large sauté pan, heat 2 tablespoons of the olive oil over high heat. Add the langoustines and remaining garlic clove, and season with salt and pepper. Pour in the Cognac and simmer until the langoustines are opaque and cooked through, about 2 minutes. Transfer the langoustines and their juices to a plate and set aside. Keep warm.

5. In the same pan, heat the remaining 1 tablespoon olive oil over medium-high heat. Add the mushrooms and season with salt and pepper. Cook until tender and browned, about 3 minutes.

6. Add the langoustines and mushrooms and any accumulated juices to the pot with the chicken and mix the ingredients gently. Continue to simmer over low heat for 15 to 20 minutes for the flavors to blend. Sprinkle with the parsley just before serving.

GUINEA HEN RAVIOLI

⟿ SERVES 6 ⟿

When it comes to cooking I have a strong preference for simple, rustic, and classic over complicated, modern, and pretentious. If I could go to only one restaurant for the rest of my life it wouldn't be a Michelin-starred one; it would be an honest bistro with straightforward dishes, prepared with the finest ingredients. Having said that, I have had many remarkable experiences in the temples of haute cuisine, and one thing I have to admit they often do well is various sorts of "French-ified" raviolis, sometimes filled with exotic mushrooms or meaty stuffings, served with inventive sauces and garnished with fresh herbs. You could say that this recipe is my attempt at being fancy. I hope I succeeded.

FOR THE STUFFING

1 WHOLE GUINEA HEN OR CHICKEN (3 POUNDS / 1.5 KG)

FINE SEA SALT AND FRESHLY GROUND BLACK PEPPER

3 TABLESPOONS EXTRA-VIRGIN OLIVE OIL, PLUS MORE FOR DRIZZLING

½ POUND / 230 G SAVOY CABBAGE, FINELY CHOPPED

2 LARGE EGGS

¼ CUP FINELY CHOPPED FRESH FLAT-LEAF PARSLEY LEAVES

¼ CUP CHOPPED FRESH CHIVES

¼ TEASPOON GRATED NUTMEG

1 MEDIUM YELLOW ONION, DICED

1 MEDIUM CARROT, DICED

1 CELERY STALK, DICED

1 BOUQUET GARNI (SEE PAGE 79)

1. **MAKE THE STUFFING.** Preheat the oven to 350°F / 180°C.

2. Put the guinea fowl in a baking dish, season generously with salt and pepper, and drizzle with olive oil. Roast for about 40 minutes. The bird will be slightly undercooked so the meat will be juicy. Set aside to cool slightly. Remove the skin and discard. Remove the bones and reserve them. Chop the meat finely and put the meat in a large bowl.

3. Add the cabbage, eggs, parsley, chives, and nutmeg to the meat and season with salt and pepper.

4. In a large pot, heat the 3 tablespoons olive oil over medium-high heat. Add the onion, carrot, celery, and guinea hen bones and cook until golden, about 5 minutes. Season lightly with salt and pepper. Add the bouquet garni and enough cold water to cover the ingredients. Cover the pot and bring the water to a boil. Reduce the heat and simmer gently for 1 hour. After 1 hour, uncover, increase the heat to high, and boil the stock until it reduces to 1 cup / 240 ml.

FOR THE PASTA DOUGH

4 CUPS / 480 G ALL-PURPOSE
FLOUR, SIFTED, PLUS MORE
AS NEEDED

5 LARGE EGGS

3 TABLESPOONS EXTRA-VIRGIN
OLIVE OIL

PINCH OF FINE SEA SALT

1 LARGE EGG YOLK

SEMOLINA FLOUR

JUICE OF ½ LEMON

4 TABLESPOONS / 60 G UNSALTED
BUTTER, CUT INTO PIECES

CHOPPED FRESH CHIVES, FOR
SERVING

5. **MEANWHILE, MAKE THE PASTA DOUGH.** Put the flour on a clean work surface and make a well in the center. Add the eggs, olive oil, and salt. Using a fork, beat the eggs and then gradually mix in the flour, using your hands when the dough is too stiff to stir. Knead with the heel of your hand, sprinkling the dough with additional flour if it gets too sticky, until it is soft and elastic, but still slightly sticky, 6 to 8 minutes. Shape into a ball and wrap in plastic wrap. Let it rest at room temperature for 30 minutes.

6. In a small bowl, mix 1 tablespoon water with the egg yolk to make an egg wash.

7. Scatter flour over a large, clean surface. With a rolling pin, roll the dough out until it is just thin enough to fit through the rollers of a pasta machine. Roll the pasta through each setting of a pasta machine until it is the thinnest it can be. Cut the dough in half. On one sheet, carefully scoop 1 teaspoon stuffing every 3 to 4 inches / 8 to 10 cm, and then brush around each mound of filling with the egg wash. Drape the second sheet of pasta over the first one, gently pushing around each filling mound with your fingers to seal and remove any air bubbles. Trim each ravioli parcel with a sharp knife or a pasta stamp of your choice to form a neat shape, whether square, oval, or round.

8. Line a baking sheet with wax paper and scatter a good amount of semolina on top. Transfer the ravioli to the baking sheet. Cover loosely with plastic wrap and place in the refrigerator.

9. Bring a large pot of salted water to a boil over medium-high heat.

10. Strain the stock through a sieve into a small saucepan. Add the lemon juice and bring to a boil over high heat. Remove from the heat and whisk in the butter until it melts and the sauce thickens.

11. Drop the ravioli into the boiling water and stir gently. The ravioli are cooked when they float to the surface, about 1½ minutes. Scoop out with a slotted spoon and transfer to warm serving plates. Top with the sauce and sprinkle with the chives. Serve immediately.

ROAST DUCK WITH CHERRIES

SERVES 4 TO 6

*C*onfit de canard has always been one of my favorite dishes and throughout my childhood I enjoyed duck in various Chinese meals, not least the most famous one, Peking duck. But duck breast or a whole roast duck, done in the French style, wasn't ever that close to my heart. Over the years, slowly but surely that has changed, and I think that by now duck has ascended to the top of the list as my favorite meat of all. It's such an interesting meat, somewhere between other birds and true red meats; sometimes I think it deserves to be called the Flavor of France. A roast duck is always special, but in early summer I love to cook it with an abundance of fresh cherries. It's an old-fashioned dish, one that calls for the finest table linens and the shiniest silver, and is best enjoyed by candlelight.

1 WHOLE DUCK
(3 TO 4 POUNDS / 1.5 TO 2 KG)

8 TABLESPOONS / 120 G UNSALTED
BUTTER, AT ROOM TEMPERATURE

FINE SEA SALT AND FRESHLY
GROUND BLACK PEPPER

5 GARLIC CLOVES, UNPEELED

A FEW SPRIGS OF FRESH THYME

A FEW SPRIGS OF FRESH ROSEMARY

1 POUND / 450 G CHERRIES,
STEMMED

1 TABLESPOON HONEY

1 TABLESPOON BALSAMIC VINEGAR

⅓ CUP / 80 ML CALVADOS

1. Preheat the oven to 375°F / 190°C.

2. Put the duck in a roasting pan, rub the skin generously with 6 tablespoons / 90 g of the butter, and season inside and out with salt and pepper. Put the whole garlic cloves, thyme, rosemary, and a small handful of the cherries inside the cavity. Roast until golden brown, cooked through, and tender, about 1 hour 20 minutes.

3. When the duck is done, let it rest for about 20 minutes to let the juices settle before carving.

4. Meanwhile, in a large saucepan, melt the remaining 2 tablespoons / 30 g butter over medium heat. Add the remaining cherries, the honey, and balsamic vinegar and shake the pan. Pour in the Calvados, light a match, and carefully ignite the liquid to flambé.

5. Place the duck on a serving platter, pour the juices all over, and scoop the remaining cherries around the bird. Serve immediately.

QUAIL STUFFED WITH FOIE GRAS

SERVES 4

To many people, cooking quail or squab sounds difficult, fancy, and somehow out of reach. The truth is: It's actually quite simple. When I throw a fairly large dinner party I find it easier to cook one or two birds per person than roast two or three larger birds and then have to carve and plate them. Most of the work can be done in advance, and the only thing that remains last minute is to make a pan sauce. Often my guests follow me to the kitchen as I am finishing up. The highlight comes when I flambé the sauce—which often results in clapping. All very eighties, in a good way.

4 QUAILS, CLEANED

FINE SEA SALT AND FRESHLY
GROUND BLACK PEPPER

4 GARLIC CLOVES

4 SMALL SPRIGS OF FRESH THYME

3 OUNCES / 85 G FOIE GRAS,
CUT INTO 4 CUBES

2 TABLESPOONS / 30 G UNSALTED
BUTTER

⅓ CUP / 80 ML CHICKEN STOCK

¼ CUP / 60 ML CALVADOS

3 TABLESPOONS CRÈME FRAÎCHE

1. Preheat the oven to 400°F / 200°C.

2. Rinse the quails and pat dry. Season inside and out with salt and pepper. Add a clove of garlic, a sprig of thyme, and a cube of foie gras to each cavity. Rub the quails all over with the butter. With kitchen twine, tie each quail around the circumference, turn it over, and tie the twine around the circumference again.

3. Put the quails in a large roasting pan, transfer to the oven, and roast until golden brown and cooked through, 20 to 25 minutes. Remove the quails from the pan and keep warm on a plate.

4. Keep all the juices in the roasting pan and set on the stove over medium-high heat. Pour in the chicken stock and simmer for 5 minutes. Season with salt and pepper as needed. Pour in the Calvados, light a match, and carefully ignite the liquid to flambé. Once the flame has died, whisk in the crème fraîche. Remove from the heat and pour the sauce into a sauce pitcher. Serve immediately with the quails.

QUAIL MILLEFEUILLE

SERVES 4

My approach to French cooking, especially since I started writing cookbooks, has always been to try to demystify the process rather than make it sound overly complicated and tedious. A quail is just a little bird that has almost the same anatomy as a chicken. Deboning it happens in much the same way. The millefeuille part just means you are layering ingredients one on top of the other—again, not too difficult, just like making a sandwich. Each bite offers a delicious yet different layer of crunch overflowing with juices. This is an all-in-one dish, no side necessary. It is an easy dish that just sounds complicated, which works in your favor when you serve it to guests. "How fancy! Did you make this?" they will say, but you'll know the secret!

4 QUAILS

EXTRA-VIRGIN OLIVE OIL

1 MEDIUM WHITE ONION, DICED

1 SMALL CARROT, PEELED AND DICED

FINE SEA SALT AND FRESHLY
GROUND BLACK PEPPER

1 BOUQUET GARNI (SEE PAGE 79)

PINCH OF GRATED NUTMEG

5 TABLESPOONS / 75 G UNSALTED
BUTTER, PLUS 2 TABLESPOONS / 30 G
MELTED BUTTER FOR THE PHYLLO

PINCH OF RABELAIS SPICE OR
ALLSPICE

½ HEAD SAVOY CABBAGE, SLICED
INTO STRIPS

4 RUSSET POTATOES, PEELED AND
VERY THINLY SLICED, PREFERABLY
USING A MANDOLINE

5 SHEETS FROZEN PHYLLO (FILO)
PASTRY, THAWED

2 TABLESPOONS RED WINE

1 BUNCH OF SPRING ONIONS
(4 OR 5), WHITE AND GREEN PARTS,
THINLY SLICED

1 BUNCH OF FRESH CHIVES,
FINELY CHOPPED

1. Cut the quail breasts off the bones and cut off the legs. Chop the quail carcasses into chunks.

2. In a large pot, heat 3 tablespoons olive oil over medium heat. Add the onion, carrot, and quail carcass pieces and cook until golden, about 5 minutes. Season lightly with salt and pepper. Add the bouquet garni, nutmeg, and enough water to just cover the ingredients. Cover the pot and simmer over medium-low heat for at least 45 minutes and up to 1 hour 30 minutes, as time allows. Uncover the pot and boil the quail stock over high heat until you have about ¾ cup / 180 ml.

3. Meanwhile, in a sauté pan, heat 1 tablespoon / 15 grams of the butter over medium heat. Season the quail breasts and legs with salt and pepper and the Rabelais spice. Add to the pan and cook until golden on each side, a few minutes per side. The meat should be very rare at this point as you want it to stay tender and keep all its juices. Set aside to cool, then slice the breast meat thinly, and, using a fork, remove all the meat from the legs.

4. Melt 2 tablespoons / 30 grams of the butter in the pan over medium heat. Add the cabbage, season with salt, and sauté for 3 minutes; it will still be slightly crunchy. Set aside in a bowl.

(recipe continues)

5. In the same pan, heat enough olive oil to cover the bottom of the pan over medium heat. Working in batches and adding additional oil as needed, cook the potatoes until golden on both sides, 1 to 2 minutes per side. Season with salt. Set aside on paper towels to absorb any excess oil.

6. Preheat the oven to 350°F / 180°C.

7. Lightly brush each phyllo pastry sheet with melted butter using a pastry brush. Cut out 20 rounds about 4½ inches / 11.5 cm in diameter.

8. Strain the quail stock through a sieve into a small saucepan (discard the solids). Bring to a boil over high heat. Add the wine and continue to boil for 2 minutes. Remove from the heat, add the remaining 2 tablespoons / 30 g butter, and whisk constantly until the butter is melted and the sauce has thickened. Season as needed with salt and pepper.

9. Line a rimmed baking sheet with parchment paper. Put 4 rounds of phyllo on the sheet, topping each with a layer of potatoes. Continue with a layer of quail, cabbage, and a few slices of spring onion. Repeat to make four layers per serving, ending with the last phyllo rounds on top. Brush with melted butter.

10. Bake until the pastry is golden and everything is hot, 8 to 10 minutes. Serve the quail millefeuilles on plates, drizzling the sauce around them and sprinkling with the chives and any remaining spring onion.

CASSOULET

SERVES 8

In the canon of French cooking there are many stars, quite a few legends and power players, but only a handful of true titans, dishes that on their own seem to preserve the food traditions of entire regions—sometimes even the whole country. Cassoulet is to French cuisine what Victor Hugo's *Les Misérables* is to the literary canon. My mother's family comes from the heartland of the southwest, near Toulouse, the birthplace of cassoulet. From time to time you can get a really good version in an excellent French bistro, especially in winter, but more often than not the best place to enjoy it is in someone's home.

I actually didn't start making cassoulet until I was in my midthirties; it just took me some time to get there. This dish requires a bit of patience and a number of good ingredients, but it doesn't require any special techniques or tricks. You may be thinking "I'll probably never make this," but I encourage you to do so some day. The recipe is here when you're ready.

1½ POUNDS / 700 G DRIED WHITE BEANS, SUCH AS HARICOTS TARBAIS

8 WHOLE CLOVES

3 LARGE YELLOW ONIONS: 2 SLICED AND 1 LEFT WHOLE

2 MEDIUM CARROTS, PEELED AND CHOPPED

1 BOUQUET GARNI (SEE PAGE 79)

10 OUNCES / 300 G COOKED GARLIC SAUSAGE (SAUCISSON À L'AIL)

7 OUNCES / 200 G SLAB BACON

2 TABLESPOONS TOMATO PASTE

FINE SEA SALT AND FRESHLY GROUND BLACK PEPPER

4 TABLESPOONS RENDERED GOOSE FAT OR OLIVE OIL

1 POUND / 450 G BONELESS LAMB SHOULDER, CUT INTO 4-INCH / 10 CM PIECES

1. Put the dried beans in a large bowl, add three times their volume of water, and let soak overnight.

2. The next day, drain and rinse the beans. Put them in a large pot and add cold water to cover by 2 inches / 5 cm. Stick the cloves into the whole onion and add to the pot along with the carrots, bouquet garni, garlic sausage, slab bacon, 1 tablespoon of the tomato paste, and 1 teaspoon salt. Give everything a big stir to combine. Bring to a boil, then reduce the heat and simmer until the beans are cooked but still hold their shape, 1 hour to 1 hour 30 minutes.

3. Meanwhile, in a deep skillet, heat 1 tablespoon of the goose fat over medium-high heat. Season the lamb on all sides with salt and pepper, add to the hot pan, and brown the meat on all sides until golden, about 4 minutes. Sprinkle with the thyme leaves and piment d'Espelette. Pour in enough water to just barely cover the meat. Bring to a boil, then reduce the heat, season with salt and pepper, and simmer for 30 minutes. Remove from the heat. Reserving the cooking liquid, drain the lamb. Set the meat and liquid aside separately.

(recipe continues)

LEAVES FROM A FEW SPRIGS OF
FRESH THYME

½ TEASPOON PIMENT D'ESPELETTE
OR MILD CHILE POWDER

6 TOULOUSE-STYLE OR OTHER
GOOD-QUALITY PORK SAUSAGES

½ POUND / 230 G BONELESS
PORK SHOULDER

5 GARLIC CLOVES, THINLY SLICED

16 OUNCES / 450 G CANNED
CHOPPED TOMATOES, DRAINED

1 TEASPOON GRATED NUTMEG

3 LARGE DUCK CONFIT LEGS

1¾ CUPS / 160 G PLAIN DRIED
BREAD CRUMBS

LEAVES FROM A FEW SPRIGS
OF FRESH FLAT-LEAF PARSLEY,
CHOPPED

4. In another skillet, heat 1 tablespoon of the goose fat over medium-high heat. Add the Toulouse sausages and cook, turning until browned on all sides, about 10 minutes. Transfer to a plate. In the same pan, sear the pork shoulder until browned on both sides, about 8 minutes.

5. In a large Dutch oven, heat the remaining 2 tablespoons goose fat over medium-high heat. Add the sliced onions and garlic and sauté until golden, about 4 minutes. Retrieve the slab bacon from the beans, chop it up into thick sticks, and add to the onions. Continue to cook for a few minutes.

6. Pick out the whole onion with the cloves and the bouquet garni from the beans and discard. Reserving their liquid, drain the beans. Set the garlic sausage aside. Return the beans to the Dutch oven, add the tomatoes, nutmeg, and remaining 1 tablespoon tomato paste, and mix all of the ingredients gently to avoid breaking the beans. Pour in enough of the reserved lamb cooking liquid and reserved bean cooking liquid to just about cover the beans. Bring the beans to a boil over medium-high heat, then reduce the heat, and simmer for 20 minutes.

7. Meanwhile, in a skillet, preferably cast iron, over medium-high heat, cook the duck legs skin side down until browned, about 6 minutes. Reserve the duck legs and newly rendered duck fat.

8. Preheat the broiler.

9. Arrange the lamb, both kinds of sausages, pork shoulder, and duck legs on top of the beans. You can slice some of the sausages and the pork if desired. Sprinkle the bread crumbs over the meats. Drizzle 2 tablespoons of the rendered duck fat from the skillet over the bread crumbs and sprinkle with the parsley. Broil until the crumbs are golden, 5 to 8 minutes. Serve immediately.

NOTES ON WINE

BY ODDUR THORISSON

RED WINE IS MY FAVORITE DRINK. That and coffee. If I had to write about coffee it would be easy and short; I know next to nothing about it. I know good coffee from bad and I know where to find the former: Italy! (And a few good places in Paris and other cities.)

I know much more about wine, which makes it harder to write about. I asked my wife for advice—it's her cookbook, after all. "Just make it short and simple, darling," she said (I added the darling part). "Nobody wants to read an overly long, overly elaborate text on wine." Nobody? Really? Maybe she's right: Wine is more fun to drink than to read about.

On the off chance that anybody might be interested, here are my thoughts on wine. But first: a disclaimer! There are no real truths about wine, only opinions, which makes wine an elusive, fascinating subject. In what follows I may state things as facts; however, most of them are only my humble opinions—which are probably neither better nor worse than anybody else's.

This is what I've learned. So far.

In this house, wine and food cannot comfortably live without each other, and we rarely serve one without the other. There are a few exceptions, and Champagne is one. Champagne is *always* an exception. (That's a fact, not just an opinion. More about that later.)

But let's start with Bordeaux wines. All wines grown around Bordeaux, the city, are called Bordeaux wines. They are split into right bank, St Émilion, Pomerol, etc., and left bank, Médoc and the Graves. Due to growing conditions and traditions, the right bank favors Merlot, the left bank Cabernet Sauvignon. Having said that, almost all red Bordeaux wines are a blend of the two with a few other grape varieties added to the mix. Some say that Médoc wines are more powerful and robust, whereas right bank wines are smoother and more elegant. I don't particularly agree with that nor does it tell the whole story.

When I lived in Iceland I drank mainly Italian wines. Odd, I know, but it would take too long to explain. Let's just say that I find Italian wines wonderful. When I

lived in Paris we drank chiefly wines from Burgundy. Let's just say that I find Burgundy wines wonderful. Since our move to Médoc more than five years ago, we almost exclusively drink Médoc (and some right bank) wines. Let's just say that I find Bordeaux wines most wonderful of all.

When I talk about wines I am mainly talking about reds; whites are a different story. Bordeaux winemakers produce some excellent Sauvignon Blanc–dominated whites. The Burgundies, though, the really good ones, are still the best whites in France, probably the world.

In the rest of the world it is common to ask for a glass of Chardonnay, or a bottle of Pinot (Noir). In France it is not. Here people ask for a glass of Chablis, a bottle of Gevrey-Chambertin. A Chablis is always a Chardonnay, a Gevrey-Chambertin always a Pinot Noir. It sounds more complicated than it is. Whereas elsewhere they talk about grapes, here we talk about regions. Burgundies are Chardonnays and Pinot Noirs; Bordeaux wines are Sauvignon Blancs, Cabernet Sauvignons, and Merlots. Other regions mix it up a little more, but not that much; each region has its go-to grapes.

Médoc, our region, is home to some of the best, most prestigious wines in the world. In 1855, the King, Napoleon III, wanted to know what wines he should drink; he wanted a guide. So they gave him one, based on price and prestige of the châteaux that were most prominent at that point in time. Whether or not those were the best wines then is by now irrelevant. It was a self-fulfilling prophecy: Wines that were classified as Grand Crus in 1855 were far more likely to command higher prices, therefore giving the châteaux more money to invest in new techniques, personnel, and publicity. On top of that they probably had the best land as well.

This is the most important question anyone asks me about Bordeaux wines: "Can you still buy a good bottle of Bordeaux for under thirty euros?" The answer is yes. Absolutely. Not a Grand Cru, but yes. The second question is: "What about the Grand Crus of Bordeaux: Are they really better, are they worth it? " Again, yes. It's a painful truth for my purse but they've had more than 150 years of an advantage.

The key to understanding the value of wine is time. Good wine needs time. Great wine needs much more time. Open two bottles of a good Bordeaux vintage, say 2010. One is an affordable option, the price of a good steak in a restaurant. The other bottle costs more, the price of good shoes. Really good shoes. Taste them both now and you might feel the former is a far better buy. Taste them again in twenty years. Then you'll understand.

France is a country of wine traditions perhaps far beyond any place on earth. Other countries make wonderful wines, but France is the only country where so many families routinely invest in cases of wine from good vintages and then put them away for much later or never. We have friends who never really drink the wine they buy; they drink the wine their grandfathers bought.

My grandfathers were Icelandic. They bought vodka, then they drank it. I have thought about starting a tradition of my own, buying wine and storing it. But I have this recurring nightmare: A grandchild of mine brings home a bunch of adolescents and they raid my cellars while I'm lying in my grave.

Mimi and I love wine. We will have cocktails out of politeness or Cognac with company. But wine is what we love, and we always serve it with food. Here are our rules of thumb (except remember, there are no rules):

CHAMPAGNE IS WONDERFUL! We always start with Champagne. A good blanc de blancs (meaning it is made only from white Chardonnay grapes) is a house favorite and goes well with food. Wine experts say that Champagne is best enjoyed from a white wineglass. A flute is too tight and inhibits the wine, a coupe too open and lets the bubbles out too quickly. This is true, so take their advice; but if the occasion and dress code call for a tux and a coupe, just remember to drink fast. Really fast.

ROSÉ IS BEST WHEN IT COMES FROM PROVENCE, is a clear pale pink, and doesn't cost too much. We drink rosé only in summer.

WE NEVER SERVE FISH WITH RED WINE. We are that old-fashioned. Most of the starters in this book go very well with a white Bordeaux (Sauvignon Blanc). So do the main fish courses, but then you might start thinking about an older white Burgundy.

THE BIGGER THE OCCASION, THE BIGGER THE BOTTLE. I'm not talking size here. There is an exception to this rule, which is that you can and should open a bottle of really good, really old wine whenever you feel like it. The food needs to be good but not necessarily fancy. A great bottle of wine, great music, a simple steak, a dog on the floor. (The music is optional. The dog is not.)

FOREST PIE

Standing alone in a deep, dark forest, surrounded by trees and complete silence, perhaps accompanied by a little white dog and holding a basket filled with freshly picked mushrooms, is one of the most magical things about living in the countryside. It's why I love autumn so much, and the pleasure only deepens when I come home with my bounty of fresh porcini or chanterelles and start cooking. It's the time of year when we abandon summer and everything becomes more earthy and moody— in a good way. This tart is my homage to Médoc in autumn, filled with intriguing scents and flavors. I reserve this tart for a special occasion, served with a big, red Médoc, as old and as good as I can get.

5 TABLESPOONS / 75 G UNSALTED BUTTER

2 SMALL YELLOW ONIONS, THINLY SLICED

FINE SEA SALT AND FRESHLY GROUND BLACK PEPPER

5 OUNCES / 150 G PORCINI OR CHANTERELLE MUSHROOMS

1 GARLIC CLOVE, FINELY CHOPPED

LEAVES FROM 2 SPRIGS OF FRESH FLAT-LEAF PARSLEY, CHOPPED

1 POUND / 450 G DUCK LEG CONFIT

5 OUNCES / 150 G PORK SAUSAGE, REMOVED FROM ITS CASING

3 LARGE EGGS

¼ CUP / 60 ML CRÈME FRAÎCHE

¼ CUP / 50 ML ARMAGNAC

LEAVES FROM 3 SPRIGS OF FRESH THYME

½ TEASPOON GRATED NUTMEG

1 POUND / 450 G FROZEN PUFF PASTRY, THAWED

5 OUNCES / 150 G DUCK FOIE GRAS, CUT INTO CHUNKS

1. Preheat the oven to 350°F / 180°C.

2. In a large sauté pan, heat 2 tablespoons / 30 g of the butter over medium heat. Add the onions and cook until soft and golden, about 5 minutes. Season with salt and pepper and transfer to a plate.

3. In the same pan, melt the remaining 3 tablespoons / 45 g butter. Add the porcini and sauté over high heat for 1 minute. Season with salt and pepper. Add the garlic and continue to cook for 1 minute. Scatter the parsley into the pan and remove from the heat.

4. Remove the skin and bones from the duck legs and discard. In a large bowl, shred the meat into bite-size pieces. Combine with the sausage meat, cooked onion and mushrooms, 2 of the eggs, the crème fraîche, Armagnac, thyme, and nutmeg.

5. Lightly roll out the puff pastry sheets and then cut out two 11-inch / 28 cm rounds. Line a 9-inch / 23 cm pie dish with one round of dough. Add the meat mixture and then scatter the chunks of foie gras all over. Season with salt and pepper. Cover with the second round of dough. Seal by pressing together the two pieces of dough with your thumbs. Cut off the excess dough, reroll it, and cut out forest-inspired figures, such as leaves (5 or 6), to decorate. Press the leaves on the dough. Lightly beat the remaining egg and brush the pie with it.

6. Bake until golden brown, 25 to 30 minutes. Let rest for 10 minutes before serving.

BLACK PEPPERED FILETS MIGNONS
WITH COGNAC

 SERVES 4

When you open a restaurant you have to ask yourself: What do people like to eat? The answer is: steak, particularly a fantastic, well-cooked, perfectly seasoned one with a peppercorn crust. At least that's what I think they like because it's one of the things I love. So for the restaurant we often offered a filet mignon, drenched in creamy Cognac sauce and served with the crispiest homemade potato chips (page 247). In other words, we put my theory to the test. Almost everybody ordered it—and when they returned they were disappointed if it wasn't on the menu. In a world of no sure bets, this is the exception.

4 BEEF FILETS MIGNONS (5 TO 8 OUNCES / 125 G TO 230 G EACH)

COARSE SEA SALT AND COARSELY GROUND BLACK PEPPER

4 TABLESPOONS VEGETABLE OIL

¼ CUP / 60 ML COGNAC

½ CUP / 120 ML BEEF STOCK

4 TABLESPOONS / 60 G UNSALTED BUTTER, CUT INTO PIECES

½ CUP / 120 ML CRÈME FRAÎCHE

1. Generously season the steaks with salt and enough pepper to cover entirely. Press the seasonings in with your hands if necessary.

2. Working in two batches, heat a large skillet, preferably cast iron, over high heat until it's very hot. Add 2 tablespoons of the oil and sear the steaks over medium-high heat until well browned and medium-rare in the center, about 2 minutes per side. Repeat with the remaining steaks and oil. Set aside on a warm plate to rest while you make the sauce.

3. Pour off any excess oil from the skillet (leave as much pepper as possible) and reduce the heat to medium. Pour in the Cognac and simmer to reduce by at least half, 2 to 3 minutes. Add the beef stock and simmer gently until slightly reduced, about 3 minutes.

4. Swirl in the butter, piece by piece; as the butter melts and is incorporated, the sauce should start to thicken. Stir in the crème fraîche and continue to heat until hot. Do not boil. When the sauce coats the back of a spoon, it's ready.

5. Return the steaks to the pan, along with any accumulated juices, and turn the steaks over in the hot sauce to coat. Transfer the steaks and sauce to a platter or plates and serve immediately.

PORK TENDERLOIN WITH PRUNES
AND RED WINE SAUCE

SERVES 4

Old-fashioned is a term that could be used to describe many dishes, but it's especially apt when describing this one, a dish that goes into my Marcel Proust category: meals I imagine he might have had at his aunt's place, in the poshest, most pretentious surroundings. While thoroughly enjoying this delicious recipe, Marcel might have made a comment like "Auntie, I can't think of a finer combination than prunes and pork, a marriage made in heaven." Afterward they might have bored themselves to death with some banal card game and then Marcel would have retreated to his chambers where he would have made everything sound even better than it was—except that the pork wouldn't need to be embellished. This would have inspired future generations to re-create this dish, followed by madeleines, *bien sûr.*

FOR THE SAUCE

2½ TABLESPOONS / 35 G UNSALTED BUTTER

1 MEDIUM CARROT, DICED

2 SHALLOTS, FINELY CHOPPED

1 BAY LEAF

LEAVES FROM 3 SPRIGS OF FRESH THYME

COARSE SEA SALT AND FRESHLY GROUND BLACK PEPPER

¾ CUP / 180 ML RED WINE

2 TABLESPOONS RED WINE VINEGAR

¼ CUP / 60 ML CHICKEN OR VEGETABLE STOCK

8 OUNCES / 230 G PRUNES, SOAKED IN WARM WATER FOR 15 MINUTES

1. **MAKE THE SAUCE.** In a medium sauté pan, heat 1 tablespoon of the butter over medium heat. Add the carrot and shallots and cook until slightly golden, about 3 minutes. Add the bay leaf and thyme, season with salt and pepper, and then add the wine and vinegar. Simmer for a few minutes to reduce slightly. Pour in the stock and bring to a low boil. Reduce the heat and simmer for 10 minutes.

2. Add the remaining 1½ tablespoons butter to the pan. Drain the prunes and add them to the sauce. Continue to simmer for 5 minutes. Season with salt and pepper.

FOR THE PORK

4 TABLESPOONS / 60 G UNSALTED
BUTTER

1 TABLESPOON EXTRA-VIRGIN
OLIVE OIL

2 POUNDS / 900 G PORK
TENDERLOIN, CUT INTO
4 EQUAL PIECES

COARSE SEA SALT AND FRESHLY
GROUND BLACK PEPPER

3 GARLIC CLOVES, UNPEELED

LEAVES FROM A FEW SPRIGS OF
FRESH FLAT-LEAF PARSLEY,
FINELY CHOPPED

3. **MEANWHILE, COOK THE PORK.** In a large sauté pan, heat the butter and olive oil over medium-high heat. Season the tenderloins on both sides with salt and pepper and add to the pan with the garlic cloves. Cook on both sides until golden and cooked through, 8 to 10 minutes.

4. Spoon off and discard any excess fat from the pan, then pour the prune sauce on top of the pork. Sprinkle with the parsley. Serve immediately.

BLACK PIG PORK CHOPS

SERVES 4

It seems like an eternity ago, but once upon a time we lived in Paris, just by the Eiffel Tower. When we decided to move to the countryside I was reluctant to give up the city that easily, and thought that if we at least stayed close, say in Normandy, things would be fine. Of course life never really works out quite that way, but in my heart I still have a special place for Normandy: the white sandy (often rainy) beaches; the cows, pigs, butter, and apple cider; the endless creamy recipes; and one of my favorite movies, *A Man and a Woman*. We ended up in the South and I wouldn't have it any other way—the weather is better; the wine is certainly better—but there are days when I wonder what might have been. That's when I cook this most iconic of *Normand* recipes, made with some of the best ingredients the region has to offer.

4 BONE-IN PORK CHOPS, 1 INCH / 2.5 CM THICK

FINE SEA SALT AND FRESHLY GROUND BLACK PEPPER

2 TABLESPOONS / 30 G UNSALTED BUTTER

4 SHALLOTS, THINLY SLICED

2 GARLIC CLOVES, UNPEELED AND SMASHED

8 SAGE LEAVES

⅔ CUP / 160 ML DRY HARD APPLE CIDER

3 TABLESPOONS CRÈME FRAÎCHE

1. Preheat the oven to 325°F / 160°C.

2. Score the pork chops on both sides and season all over with salt and pepper.

3. In a large sauté pan, heat the butter over medium-high heat. Add the shallots and cook for 3 minutes. Add the pork chops and garlic cloves, reduce the heat to medium, and cook just until the juices run clear, about 7 minutes per side.

4. Transfer the pork chops to an ovenproof dish, put the sage leaves on top, and spoon the pan drippings over all. Put in the oven to keep warm.

5. Increase the heat under the pan to high and pour in the cider. Boil for 2 minutes to reduce. Add the crème fraîche, stir until thickened, and remove from the heat.

6. Pour the sauce on top of the chops and serve.

MONKFISH STEW WITH SAFFRON

SERVES 4

When I was writing the menu for our pop-up restaurant, I was conscious of wanting to present fish dishes as alternatives to all the meat I already knew would be on offer. I realized that we'd have a lot of oysters and at some point we'd have scallops and mussels and probably some crabmeat. These are all favorites of mine. I also wanted a classic whitefish dish with a rich and creamy sauce to go with a crisp, dry white wine. In the end I decided on monkfish, which may be the single most satisfying whitefish there is, and paired it with saffron, a match made in food heaven. Some boiled potatoes are nice with this, too.

3 TABLESPOONS EXTRA-VIRGIN
OLIVE OIL

2 POUNDS MONKFISH, SLICED
1 INCH / 2.5 CM THICK

FINE SEA SALT AND FRESHLY
GROUND BLACK PEPPER

2 MEDIUM SHALLOTS,
THINLY SLICED

2 MEDIUM CARROTS, PEELED AND
THINLY SLICED

1 MEDIUM LEEK, WHITE PART ONLY,
THINLY SLICED

LEAVES FROM A FEW SPRIGS OF
FRESH THYME

¼ TEASPOON SAFFRON THREADS

⅓ CUP / 80 ML WHITE WINE

¼ CUP / 60 ML CRÈME FRAÎCHE

10 FRESH BASIL LEAVES

1. In a large sauté pan, heat 1 tablespoon of the olive oil over medium heat. Season the fish with salt and pepper. Cook the monkfish in the hot pan on both sides until golden, 2 to 3 minutes per side. Set aside on a plate.

2. In a large Dutch oven, heat the remaining 2 tablespoons olive oil over medium heat. Add the shallots and cook for 2 minutes. Add the carrots, leek, thyme, and saffron threads and continue to cook for 3 minutes. Pour in the white wine and boil to reduce by half. Add the monkfish with any accumulated juices and season everything with salt and pepper. Pour in ⅓ cup / 80 ml water and bring to a simmer. Reduce the heat to low, cover, and let simmer for 20 minutes.

3. Just before serving, add the crème fraîche and stir gently. Scatter the basil leaves on top.

TURBOT WITH VIN JAUNE SAUCE

~ SERVES 4 ~

I always make a big fuss about *vin jaune*, the famous liquid gold that comes from the Jura region. In a way I've become an unpaid ambassador for the winemakers. Best described as tasting somewhere between white wine and sherry, it makes a marvelous pairing with fresh walnuts and Comté cheese, also from the Jura region. It is in cooking, however, that *vin jaune* really shines. I love to prepare fish simply—a few herbs, butter or oil. Adding *vin jaune* takes the dish, in one simple step, to another level. I almost feel I cannot take proper credit for a dish made with *vin jaune*; the acclaim belongs to the wine.

3 TABLESPOONS / 45 G UNSALTED BUTTER

1 LARGE TURBOT (ABOUT 3 POUNDS / 1.4 G), SCALED AND GUTTED

COARSE SEA SALT AND FRESHLY GROUND BLACK PEPPER

FOR THE SAUCE

1 TABLESPOON / 15 G UNSALTED BUTTER

1 SHALLOT, THINLY SLICED

⅔ CUP / 160 ML VIN JAUNE DU JURA OR DRY SHERRY

FINE SEA SALT AND FRESHLY GROUND BLACK PEPPER

⅔ CUP / 160 ML HEAVY CREAM

LEAVES FROM A FEW SPRIGS OF FRESH TARRAGON

1. Preheat the oven to 450°F / 230°C.

2. In a large sauté pan, heat the butter over medium heat. Season the fish on both sides with coarse salt and pepper. When the butter is sizzling, add the fish and sear on both sides until golden, 2 to 3 minutes per side; the fish will finish cooking in the oven.

3. Put the fish in a large baking dish and transfer to the oven. Roast until just cooked through, 15 to 20 minutes. Remove from the oven.

4. **MEANWHILE, MAKE THE SAUCE.** In a saucepan, heat the butter over medium-high heat. Add the shallot and sauté for 3 minutes. Pour in the wine, season with fine salt and pepper, and simmer to reduce until slightly thickened, about 5 minutes. Pour in the cream and continue to simmer for 3 minutes. The sauce should coat the back of a spoon. Pass the sauce through a sieve.

5. Serve the fish topped with the sauce and tarragon.

SEA SCALLOPS WITH CAULIFLOWER PURÉE AND CAPERS

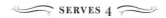

When I was working on my first book, heavily pregnant and braving the icy temperatures of New York in early March, Rica, my editor, invited me to her home for dinner. I didn't know Rica very well yet (now I do), and so I wasn't sure exactly what to expect. But I did know that her husband, Cyrille, a Frenchman from Brittany, is a pedigreed chef with experience in the finest restaurants, and that they had met working together at the celebrated restaurant Daniel many years before. Let's just say I was expecting good food. What I didn't expect was that the food would be *so* good, the evening *so* pleasant, that I'd be asking them for permission to use one of the recipes in my next cookbook (this one)—or that we would all be cooking this dish together at my restaurant in Médoc the following August. Now I'm starting to expect many more meals together—my husband takes this one step further and is expecting their son to marry one of our many daughters. As for me, I can't see that far into the future yet, but a wedding party of many cooks in Médoc has a nice ring to it.

1 NAVEL ORANGE

1 HEAD CAULIFLOWER

6½ TABLESPOONS / 90 G UNSALTED BUTTER

20 LARGE SEA SCALLOPS

FINE SEA SALT AND FRESHLY GROUND BLACK PEPPER

1 TABLESPOON EXTRA-VIRGIN OLIVE OIL

⅓ CUP / 80 ML CHICKEN STOCK

2 TABLESPOONS WHITE WINE

2 TABLESPOONS DRAINED CAPERS

A HANDFUL OF FRESH FLAT-LEAF PARSLEY LEAVES

1. Grate the zest from the orange and set the zest aside. Slice off the top and bottom of the orange with a knife and then follow the curve of the fruit to remove the peel and white pith all around. Working over a bowl, slice between the membranes to remove the orange segments. Cut each segment into a few pieces and set aside in the bowl.

2. Bring a pot of salted water to a boil. Break the cauliflower into florets. Add the florets to the boiling water and cook until the cauliflower is fork-tender, about 10 minutes. Try not to overcook it or the purée will be gelatinous instead of smooth. Drain and then purée in a blender or food processor with 3½ tablespoons / 45 g of the butter. Keep warm.

3. Pat the scallops dry with paper towels. Season with salt and pepper. In a large sauté pan, heat 2 tablespoons / 30 g of the butter with the olive oil over high heat. When the butter starts to foam, swirl the pan constantly until the color turns light brown. Add the scallops and sear on each side until browned and barely cooked in the center, 3 to 4 minutes total.

4. Meanwhile, in a small saucepan, bring the chicken stock to a boil over high heat. Add the wine and continue to boil for a few minutes. Remove from the heat and swirl in the remaining 1 tablespoon / 15 g butter, the capers, and orange segments and any juice.

5. Spoon the cauliflower purée onto shallow bowls or plates and top with the scallops. Spoon the caper sauce on top and around the scallops. Sprinkle the orange zest and parsley over the top. Serve immediately.

CRAB FEUILLETÉ

SERVES 4

When I lived in Paris and really wanted to indulge, I'd go to one of the city's famous brasseries and order myself a big seafood platter. I loved the shrimp but the crab was always my favorite. It takes a bit of work to get to the meat, but it's always worth it, and I can't think of a better way to spend a Saturday lunch. Here in Médoc we frequently buy *tourteau* claws at the market and often enjoy them simply with homemade aïoli (page 252) and freshly baked rye bread. This little recipe is a slightly more elegant way to serve crabmeat, and I love the combination of the nuttiness of the crab, the acidity of the apple, the flakiness of the pastry, and the richness of the cream. This dish screams for a nice glass of white wine, and it's so good that you have to make very large *feuilletés* per person.

8 OUNCES / 230 G FROZEN PUFF PASTRY, THAWED

½ TEASPOON SAFFRON THREADS

1 TABLESPOON / 15 G UNSALTED BUTTER

2 SHALLOTS, THINLY SLICED

¾ CUP / 180 ML CRÈME FRAÎCHE

½ POUND / 230 G PICKED CRABMEAT

FINE SEA SALT AND FRESHLY GROUND BLACK PEPPER

1 GRANNY SMITH APPLE

1 TABLESPOON FRESH LEMON JUICE

1 BUNCH OF FRESH TENDER HERB LEAVES, SUCH AS CHERVIL, BASIL, OR PARSLEY

1 TEASPOON NIGELLA SEEDS

1. Preheat the oven to 350°F / 180°C. Line a baking sheet with parchment paper.

2. Roll out the puff pastry slightly and cut out 4 rounds 3 to 5 inches / 7.5 to 12.5 cm in diameter. Prick the pastry all over with a fork, place on the lined baking sheet, leaving room between the rounds, and cover with another piece of parchment paper. Set a second baking sheet on top to keep the pastry from puffing up too much. Bake for 10 minutes. Remove the second baking sheet and the top sheet of parchment paper and bake until golden, another 5 minutes. Set aside on a wire rack to cool.

3. In a small bowl, dissolve the saffron threads in 2 teaspoons hot water.

4. In a sauté pan, heat the butter over medium heat. Add the shallots and cook until golden, about 3 minutes. Set aside to cool. Add the crème fraîche, saffron (along with the liquid), and crabmeat and season with salt and pepper.

5. Slice the apple very thinly, preferably using a mandoline. Rub the apple slices with the lemon juice to keep them from discoloring.

6. Arrange a few slices of apple on top of each round of pastry, creating a flower shape, then spoon the crab mixture on top and decorate with the herb leaves. Sprinkle some nigella seeds all over and serve.

SUNDAY SUPPERS EN FAMILLE

COMTÉ, HAM, *and*
WALNUT FEUILLETÉ *185*

ROAST CHICKEN *with*
CHESTNUTS *and* **CABBAGE** *186*

POULE-AU-POT *188*

OLD-FASHIONED SUMMER
VEAL ROAST *191*

PORK SHOULDER GRILLED
over **GRAPEVINE BRANCHES** *194*

WINE HARVEST POT-AU-FEU *195*

COD BRANDADE *198*

MUSSELS STUFFED *with*
SAUSAGE *in* **TOMATO SAUCE** *201*

BECAUSE WE LIVE in a world that moves at a faster pace than ever before in history, sitting down to dinner has never felt more important. No matter what kind of day everybody has had, we always try to have dinner together. It's not at a fixed hour (we're not that organized), but nevertheless it's something we do almost every day of the year. Sometimes these dinners happen in one of our many dining rooms (one of the perks of living in a house that is sometimes also a restaurant), but most often we eat together at the big kitchen table, which doubles as prep station and dinner table. These family meals aren't necessarily fancy, but we always try to make them tasty and fun. On weekends, or generally when I have time, the whole day could be a prelude leading up to the big moment, a trip to the market that turns into a cooking feast and culminates in culinary glory. Other days I might make a simple soup, fry some eggs, or roll out the cold cuts and cheeses. It's where we try (*try*) to teach the children table manners, but even more important, it's where matters big and small are discussed, plans are made—like family briefings . . . with food. "Have you all finished your homework?" Check. "Why was Hudson mean to his sisters? Wait, oh, why were they mean to him?" "Who broke the doorknob in the living room? Nobody? Must have been the ghosts again, then."

Our children, especially the youngest ones, have a favorite topic. It's called "What's for dessert?" Every single night Gaïa and Louise sit at the edges of their seats, trying desperately to prevent the words from escaping their little red lips. Their father, who eats more slowly and more, period, than they do, gives them a look that says, *nobody mentions dessert while the rest of us are still having the main course.* That's when they make a note to self to find a spouse who agrees to start the meal with dessert. I tend to side with the girls, albeit silently. I'm the impatient gourmand; my husband is the one who relishes delayed gratification. I know he's right, sort of. Over the years we've worked out a compromise: If he takes too long, we just go for it!

Every night is like a shorter version of life. Oddur and I set things up, sometimes with the help of little hands, and for a while we share a moment. Then the kids fly away one by one, and finally it's just the two of us, having a last sip of wine, listening to music. Because I usually cook, I tend to escape and leave him with the dishes and the dogs.

Then we start again.

COMTÉ, HAM, AND WALNUT FEUILLETÉ

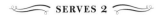

SERVES 2

If I were teaching at a French cooking school, this dish would be on the curriculum; it's the perfect crowd-pleaser, and it uses so many wonderful French ingredients. Take the best cheese and ham you can find. Make a velvety béchamel sauce. Add some moist, tender walnuts just out of the shell. Wrap everything in puff pastry, one of the most agreeable inventions of French cuisine, and bake it. I knew you'd like it.

2 TABLESPOONS PLUS 1 TEASPOON /
35 G UNSALTED BUTTER

3 TABLESPOONS ALL-PURPOSE
FLOUR

¼ TEASPOON GRATED NUTMEG

FINE SEA SALT AND FRESHLY
GROUND BLACK PEPPER

1 CUP / 250 ML WHOLE MILK

1 SHALLOT, THINLY SLICED

⅓ CUP / 50 G WALNUTS, CHOPPED

8 OUNCES / 230 G FROZEN PUFF
PASTRY, THAWED

1 TEASPOON WHOLE-GRAIN
MUSTARD

⅔ CUP / 100 G GRATED COMTÉ
CHEESE

5 OUNCES / 150 G SLICED HAM

1 LARGE EGG YOLK

1. Preheat the oven to 400°F / 200°C. Line a baking sheet with parchment paper.

2. In a small saucepan, melt 2 tablespoons of the butter over medium heat. Whisk in the flour until the mixture thickens. Add the nutmeg, season with salt and pepper, and gradually whisk in the milk and simmer, whisking until thickened, up to 5 minutes. Set the béchamel sauce aside to cool.

3. In a sauté pan, heat the remaining 1 teaspoon butter over medium heat. Add the shallot and cook until slightly golden, about 3 minutes. Add the walnuts and cook for 1 minute more.

4. Cut the puff pastry into two 9 × 5-inch / 23 × 12.5 cm rectangles. Place one rectangle of pastry on the lined baking sheet. Spread ½ teaspoon of the mustard in a thin layer over the pastry. Spread with one-third of the béchamel sauce, half of the cheese, half of the ham, and half of the walnut mixture. Repeat the layering. Finish with a layer of béchamel sauce and top with the second pastry rectangle. Seal to the bottom rectangle by pinching together the edges of the pastry.

5. Beat the egg yolk with a little water and use it to glaze the top with a pastry brush. Using a knife, cut a little round hole in the middle of the pastry to let the steam escape. You can decorate the top with cut pieces of puff pastry (leaves, for example) or lightly score a diamond pattern on top.

6. Bake the *feuilleté* in the oven until golden brown, 20 to 25 minutes. Slice and serve hot.

ROAST CHICKEN WITH CHESTNUTS AND CABBAGE

SERVES 6

I have a few staple roast chicken recipes that I use all the time. One is simple, with thyme and lemon; another one is rich, with a lot of crème fraîche and delicious herbs. I didn't really need a third one, but I came up with this recipe because I was looking for something festive, almost like a pheasant or guinea hen—which means chestnuts, my favorite. Finally, I needed a way to use up all that cabbage that my husband keeps growing and buying (because he says it's the most photogenic vegetable in the world). This chicken dish is the answer.

FOR THE CHICKEN

1 WHOLE CHICKEN (3½ POUNDS / 1.5 KG)

4 TABLESPOONS / 60 G SALTED BUTTER

FINE SEA SALT AND FRESHLY GROUND BLACK PEPPER

4 GARLIC CLOVES, UNPEELED

1 BUNCH OF FRESH THYME

1 SMALL ONION, HALVED

1 BAY LEAF

8 PEELED COOKED CHESTNUTS (BOTTLED OR VACUUM-PACKED)

FOR THE CABBAGE

1 HEAD SAVOY CABBAGE (DARK GREEN LEAVES DISCARDED), CUT INTO 1-INCH / 2.5 CM STRIPS

20 OUNCES / 570 G PEELED COOKED CHESTNUTS (BOTTLED OR VACUUM-PACKED)

5 TABLESPOONS / 75 G UNSALTED BUTTER

FINE SEA SALT AND FRESHLY GROUND BLACK PEPPER

⅓ CUP / 80 ML CHICKEN STOCK

⅓ CUP / 80 ML DRY WHITE WINE

1. **ROAST THE CHICKEN.** Preheat the oven to 350°F / 180°C. Take the chicken out of the refrigerator at least 30 minutes before cooking.

2. Rub the chicken with the salted butter and season generously both inside and out with salt and pepper. Put the garlic cloves, thyme, onion halves, bay leaf, and chestnuts in the cavity. Put the chicken in a roasting pan and roast for 50 minutes.

3. Transfer the chicken to a big plate; it will not be fully cooked just yet and will be returned to the oven later, so leave the oven on but increase the temperature to 400°F / 200°C.

4. **MAKE THE CABBAGE.** Keep all the fat and juices in the roasting pan and add the cabbage, chestnuts, and 4 tablespoons / 60 g of the unsalted butter. Season with salt and pepper and toss everything together. Return to the oven and roast for 10 minutes.

5. Pour in the stock and wine and stir to combine. Brush the chicken with the remaining 1 tablespoon / 15 g butter to gloss the skin and return to the pan. Return the pan to the oven and roast until the chicken is golden brown and cooked through, 10 to 15 minutes.

6. Let the chicken rest for 15 minutes before serving with the cabbage and chestnuts.

POULE-AU-POT

SERVES 6

Some things sound better in French than in English. Chicken in a pot or even boiled chicken isn't that tempting. I remember the first time I made this dish for my husband, in our early days in Paris. "Aren't you supposed to at least brown the chicken first?" he asked. I just gave him a look—the kind of look that doesn't need to be translated. Sometime later in the day, when he was enjoying the *poule-au-pot* immensely, he gave me a different look, one that said, "You were right, I was wrong." It's my favorite kind of look. In fact, he likes this dish so much that he wants you to know that this is his favorite photograph in the book.

Poule-au-pot is such a national treasure, and there are many different versions of it. This one is the result of years of experimenting; but to give credit where credit's due, it owes much to my dear friend Florence's mother, who meticulously rubs the inside of the chicken skin with a garlic mixture. There is more to this dish than meets the eye: I call it country chic.

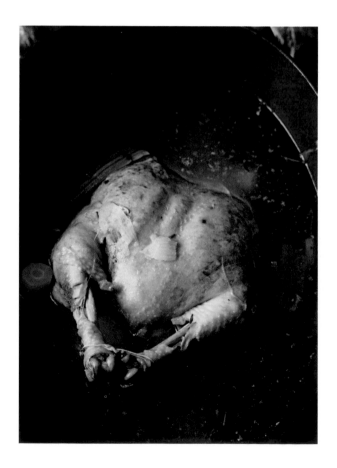

FOR THE CHICKEN

4 OUNCES / 110 G STALE BREAD

⅓ CUP / 80 ML WHOLE MILK

5 OUNCES / 150 G SLICED HAM,
PREFERABLY BAYONNE, FINELY
CHOPPED

5 OUNCES / 150 G BACON,
FINELY CHOPPED

2 SHALLOTS, FINELY CHOPPED

4 GARLIC CLOVES, 1 FINELY
CHOPPED AND 3 LEFT WHOLE

2 LARGE EGGS, LIGHTLY BEATEN

LEAVES FROM 1 SMALL BUNCH
OF FRESH FLAT-LEAF PARSLEY,
CHOPPED

1 WHOLE CHICKEN
(3½ POUNDS / 1.5 KG)

FINE SEA SALT AND FRESHLY
GROUND BLACK PEPPER

2 MEDIUM LEEKS, WHITE PART ONLY

2 MEDIUM CARROTS, PEELED

1 CELERY STALK

1 ONION, STUDDED WITH
8 WHOLE CLOVES

1 BOUQUET GARNI (SEE PAGE 79)

FOR THE MUSHROOM SAUCE

8 TABLESPOONS / 120 G UNSALTED
BUTTER

10 OUNCES / 300 G WHITE
MUSHROOMS

1 MEDIUM WHITE ONION,
THINLY SLICED

FINE SEA SALT AND FRESHLY
GROUND BLACK PEPPER

¾ CUP / 90 G ALL-PURPOSE FLOUR

1. **PREPARE THE CHICKEN.** Soak the bread in the milk for 10 minutes.

2. In a large bowl, combine the ham, bacon, shallots, chopped garlic, eggs, and parsley. Remove the giblets from the cavity of the chicken. Finely chop the gizzard and liver and add to the bowl. Squeeze excess milk from the bread and crumble the bread into the bowl. Season with salt and pepper and mix well to combine.

3. Gently lift the skin away from the breast meat on each side of the chicken, being careful not to tear the skin. Gently arrange the stuffing, with the help of a small spoon or your fingers, under the skin on top of the breast meat. Scoop any leftover stuffing inside the chicken's cavity and tie the chicken legs together with kitchen twine.

4. In a Dutch oven or other large pot, pour in enough cold water to cover the chicken (3 to 4 quarts / liters) and add the leeks, carrots, celery, clove-studded onion, bouquet garni, and the whole garlic cloves. Season with salt and pepper. Bring to a boil. Carefully add the chicken to the pot, making sure it's entirely covered in liquid (if not, add more water as needed). Cover and reduce the heat to low. Simmer very gently until the chicken is cooked through, 1 hour 15 minutes to 1 hour 30 minutes.

5. **MAKE THE MUSHROOM SAUCE.** In a large sauté pan, heat 2 tablespoons / 30 g of the butter over medium-high heat. Add the mushrooms and onion and sauté until golden, 4 to 5 minutes. Season with salt and pepper. Remove from the heat.

6. In a medium saucepan, melt the remaining 6 tablespoons / 90 g butter over medium heat. Off the heat, add the flour all at once, mix well with a whisk, and return to medium-low heat. Cook, whisking, until the color turns golden, about 8 minutes. Whisk in ⅓ cup / 80 ml of the chicken cooking liquid to thicken the sauce.

7. Scrape the mushroom mixture into the sauce, adding a little more chicken stock if needed to thin. Season with salt and pepper as needed.

8. Remove the chicken from the broth and set aside to cool for 3 minutes. Cut the chicken into pieces and remove the stuffing from the cavity. Slice the stuffing into rounds. Arrange the chicken pieces, stuffing slices, and vegetables on a serving platter and drizzle with a little of the broth. Serve with the mushroom sauce on the side.

OLD-FASHIONED SUMMER VEAL ROAST

SERVES 6

When our restaurant is open in summer, guests enter through the side of the house and go through what we like to call the *boucherie,* or the butcher shop, named after a very large butcher's table we found at the antiques fair in Bordeaux some years ago. When they enter, my husband usually offers a sparkling glass of Champagne and some charcuterie to go with it. A few times in summer, for a few lucky days, guests might notice a delectable aroma emanating from the Bordeaux-colored stove in the corner. And if the smell were better than anything you could have possibly expected to be served that night, you could be sure that we were making this veal roast that my family loves, one we make only in summer and only with fresh, multicolored cherry tomatoes from our own vegetable garden. These are good memories.

4 TABLESPOONS / 60 G UNSALTED BUTTER

2 MEDIUM YELLOW ONIONS, SLICED

8 OUNCES / 230 G PANCETTA, CUT INTO THIN MATCHSTICKS

2¾ POUNDS / 1.3 KG BONE-IN VEAL SHOULDER ROAST

3 SMALL CARROTS, THINLY SLICED

2 CELERY STALKS, THINLY SLICED

COARSE SEA SALT AND FRESHLY GROUND BLACK PEPPER

1 BOUQUET GARNI (SEE PAGE 79)

2 CUPS / 480 ML DRY WHITE WINE

15 PLUM TOMATOES

⅓ CUP / 80 ML BEEF OR CHICKEN STOCK

4 GARLIC CLOVES, UNPEELED

1. Preheat the oven to 325°F / 160°C.

2. In a large Dutch oven, melt the butter over medium heat. Add the onions and sauté until soft but not browned, about 3 minutes. Add the pancetta and continue to cook for 3 minutes. Add the veal and brown on all sides, about 8 minutes. Add the carrots and celery, season with salt and pepper, and throw in the bouquet garni. Pour in the wine and mix all the ingredients together. Bring to a simmer, add the tomatoes, beef stock, and garlic cloves, and cover the pot.

3. Transfer the pot to the oven and braise until cooked through and tender, 1 hour 30 minutes to 2 hours.

4. Cut the veal into slices and serve with the vegetables and pan juices.

PORK SHOULDER GRILLED
OVER GRAPEVINE BRANCHES

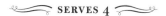

We live and breathe amongst the vines of Médoc, where some of the finest wines in the world are made. Wherever we go we traverse a sea of vineyards before we reach our destination. That's my favorite part of the journey. Traveling through the vines. And it doesn't matter what time of year it is; each season has its own glory. The brightly burning yellows and reds of autumn precede the moment when the leaves disappear and the vines stand naked. In January, pruning season commences and the finer branches (*sarments de vigne*) are tied up in bundles and trans-ferred to a cozy place for drying. That's when we try to get our hands on as many bundles as possible, when they are plentiful. After a few months, in late spring or early summer, the vine branches are dry enough to use for grilling.

We are lucky enough to have a huge fireplace in our kitchen, one of the perks of the house, and we cook in it all the time. Grilled meat gets infused with the smoke from the grapevines, and the taste is unlike any other. When I host cooking work-shops in my house, I always make sure to do a Médoc-style barbecue at least once, and everybody loves it. My favorite part is when they discuss how they could re-create this sort of cooking at home with a backyard grill and local wine branches. These delicious slices of marbled pork shoulder, which I season heavily with garlic, are a great place to start.

1½ POUNDS / 650 G BONELESS
PORK SHOULDER, CUT INTO
4 SLICES

FINE SEA SALT AND FRESHLY
GROUND BLACK PEPPER

1 TABLESPOON / 15 G UNSALTED
BUTTER

2 GARLIC CLOVES, THINLY SLICED

1. Prepare a medium-hot fire in a grill. Add dried grapevine branches, if desired, to increase the smoky flavor.

2. Season the meat with salt and pepper. Grill the pork until browned, golden, and cooked through, about 7 minutes on each side.

3. Just before serving, spread the butter over the pork and scatter the sliced garlic on top.

WINE HARVEST POT-AU-FEU

~ SERVES 6 ~

Sometimes in winter when I'm buying vegetables at the market, I see elderly men in old sweaters buying vegetables. They always buy the same things: potatoes, leeks, carrots, turnips, parsnips, some cabbage. I also know that when they get home, they or their wives all cook the same things, too: *blanquette de veau* or *pot-au-feu*. It's hard to imagine a more familiar dish than *pot-au-feu*, a humble but delicious meat stew. Sometimes I even forget it exists; there are so many other, more exciting, recipes to cook. But once in a while I cook this classic and I'm always so happy I did. A dimly lit kitchen, a hot *pot-au-feu* in a cast-iron pot in the middle of the table, a big jar of strong mustard, a carafe of simple table wine, some candles. As they say, *comme autrefois*.

2 POUNDS / 900 G VEAL SHANK

1½ POUNDS / 750 G TENDER BEEF
SHOULDER OR BRISKET

2 POUNDS / 900 G BONELESS BEEF
BRISKET, ROLLED

8 WHOLE CLOVES

2 LARGE YELLOW ONIONS, UNPEELED
AND HALVED

1 POUND / 450 G CARROTS, PEELED
AND HALVED

1 POUND / 450 G LEEKS, WHITE
AND PALE-GREEN PARTS, CUT INTO
CHUNKS

3 CELERY STALKS, HALVED

1 TURNIP, PEELED AND CUT INTO
CHUNKS

2 GARLIC CLOVES, SLICED

1 BOUQUET GARNI (SEE PAGE 79)

1 BAY LEAF

COARSE SEA SALT AND FRESHLY
GROUND BLACK PEPPER

5 MEDIUM RUSSET POTATOES, HALVED

½ HEAD SAVOY CABBAGE, SLICED
INTO LARGE STRIPS

CORNICHONS, FOR SERVING

DIJON MUSTARD, FOR SERVING

1. Individually tie the veal shank, beef shoulder, and brisket firmly with kitchen twine so the pieces keep their shape during cooking. Put them in a very large pot and add enough water to cover. Bring the water to a boil over high heat. As soon as the water boils, remove from the heat and discard the water. Remove all of the pieces of meat, set aside on a large plate, and rinse the pot to get rid of any traces of scum. Return the meat to the pot.

2. Stick the cloves into the onion halves. Toss them into the pot along with the carrots, leeks, celery, turnip, garlic, bouquet garni, and bay leaf and cover with cold water. Season with salt and pepper. Bring the water to a boil over medium-high heat. Cover the pot, reduce the heat, and simmer for 3 hours, checking the pot from time to time to skim off any scum from the surface and to add water if necessary to cover the ingredients.

3. Add the potatoes and cabbage and continue to simmer until they are tender, about 45 minutes. Adjust the seasoning if necessary.

4. Take out the meat and vegetables and transfer to a large serving plate. Slice the meat. Spoon a few ladles of the broth into bowls, add some meat and vegetables, and serve with the cornichons, mustard, and some salt.

COD BRANDADE

SERVES 4 TO 6

I don't think there is a fishmonger in France who doesn't have his version of *brandade de morue*. It's one of the all-time great French bistro classics and I've been ordering it in restaurants all my life. I used to make the more typical version, which incorporates potatoes into the mix; but while that version is brilliant, I have come to love this even more authentic approach where the cod shines unadulterated. And instead, I serve the potatoes on the side: I sauté them until they are golden and slightly crispy, drench them in garlic, and enjoy them on their own. The only drawback to this dish is that salt cod needs to be soaked a day in advance, so that calls for some planning—not one of my fortes, I must admit.

1 POUND / 900 G SALT COD

1 CUP / 240 ML WHOLE MILK

¼ CUP / 60 ML HEAVY CREAM

1 CUP / 250 ML EXTRA-VIRGIN
OLIVE OIL

2 GARLIC CLOVES, MINCED

FRESHLY GROUND BLACK PEPPER

LEAVES FROM 6 SPRIGS OF FRESH
FLAT-LEAF PARSLEY, CHOPPED

JUICE OF ½ LEMON

1. Put the salt cod in a large bowl and cover entirely with cold water. Refrigerate for 24 hours, changing the water at least 6 times.

2. Drain the cod, cut in half, and transfer to a large saucepan. Pour in ½ cup / 120 ml of the milk and add just enough water to cover the fish. Bring to a low boil over medium heat. Skim the surface, cover, and let sit off the heat for 10 minutes. Drain the cod, discarding the cooking liquid. Remove the skin and bones using a small fork and discard.

3. In a food processor, combine the cod, remaining ½ cup / 120 ml milk, the cream, olive oil, and garlic. Process until nearly smooth, a few seconds. You still want a few chunks here and there, but on the small side. The consistency should not be too thick or too liquid, just a soft, smooth mixture. Season generously with pepper.

4. Transfer to a bowl, add the parsley and lemon juice, and toss everything together with two spoons.

MUSSELS STUFFED WITH SAUSAGE IN TOMATO SAUCE

SERVES 4

When my mother was young, she lived with her widowed mother and older sister in Moissac, a small town in the south of France, not far from Toulouse. In the summer they would visit their grandmother, Augustine, who spent her summers on a houseboat near Sète, a charming seaside town, close to Montpellier. My great-grandmother was an excellent cook, and my mother has told me these are some of her happiest childhood memories. While a love of cooking didn't really rub off on my mother, her sister Francine (or Taty as I call her) caught the bug. In my last book, *A Kitchen in France*, I included Taty's recipe for fava bean soup; I love preserving family recipes. When she phoned me with her choice for this book, she was very emotional. "Your great-grandmother would have been so proud," she said, to see this recipe in a cookbook. So here is the simple seafood recipe that made two little girls who had just lost their father happy on a houseboat in the south of France, once upon a time.

6 POUNDS MUSSELS

4 TABLESPOONS / 60 ML
EXTRA-VIRGIN OLIVE OIL

2¼ POUNDS / 1 KG PORK SAUSAGE,
CASINGS REMOVED

4 GARLIC CLOVES, FINELY CHOPPED

⅓ CUP / 80 ML RED WINE

2 CANS (14 OUNCES / 400 G EACH)
CHOPPED TOMATOES

FINE SEA SALT AND FRESHLY
GROUND BLACK PEPPER

4 TABLESPOONS / 60 G UNSALTED
BUTTER

6 SHALLOTS, FINELY CHOPPED

1 BOUQUET GARNI (SEE PAGE 79)

2 CUPS / 500 ML WHITE WINE

LEAVES FROM 1 BUNCH OF FRESH
FLAT-LEAF PARSLEY,
FINELY CHOPPED

1. To clean the mussels, put them in a large bowl with 4 quarts / 4 liters cold water. Soak for 20 minutes so the mussels disgorge any sand. Drain the mussels and remove the beards by tearing them out with your fingers. Discard any broken mussels or those that aren't properly closed. Rinse them and soak them one more time for 10 minutes.

2. In a large skillet, heat the olive oil over medium heat. Add the sausage meat in batches and cook, breaking it up with a wooden spoon, until it starts to brown, 8 to 10 minutes. Return all of the sausage to the pan, add the garlic, and cook for another 2 minutes. Pour in the red wine and simmer for 2 minutes. Stir in the tomatoes and their juices and season with salt and pepper. Remove from the heat and keep warm.

3. In a large pot, melt the butter over medium-high heat. Add the shallots and fry gently until golden, about 4 minutes. Add the bouquet garni, white wine, and salt and pepper to taste and bring to a boil. Add the mussels, cover tightly with a lid, and simmer over medium heat for 5 minutes, or until the shells open. Discard any that do not open.

4. Remove the mussels from the pot with a slotted spoon and pile into a large bowl. Add half of the mussel cooking liquid and pour the sausage mixture on top. Toss gently to mix. Sprinkle with the parsley and serve.

STAFF MEALS

IN THE TWO last years before leaving Paris for Médoc, I worked on a restaurant guide of the city that included a lot of behind-the-scenes glimpses and discoveries. I became fascinated with staff meals at restaurants, often so rustic and hurried, always so tasty looking and inviting. I enjoyed seeing the cooks and waitstaff settling around a table in the restaurant just before service and having a moment of their own, eating a meal that might not have compared in elegance or inventiveness to what they were about to serve others, but a meal that would give most comfort food a run for its money. There would be banter and laughter, practical jokes and, sometimes, for better or worse, inappropriate humor. A good word for it would be camaraderie, the essence of a simple meal shared. When we decided to open our little pop-up restaurant for a month in August, it was one of the things I most looked forward to: sitting with my apron on, having a homey meal with my team, the calm before the storm.

In reality it didn't always turn out that way. More often than not, when we had reservations only in the evening and not for lunch but had gathered earlier in the day to prep, one of us would cook something delicious for the team, and for a little while we would sit, sip wine (mostly rosé—and April drank most of it), and enjoy simple food, things that energized us, made us feel happy and strong. But at night, despite good intentions, we just weren't the pros we thought we were. Usually, when evening service neared, we were lucky if the food for the guests was remotely ready, let alone something for us. There would be nibbles of sausages, and Oddur kept the cooks in wine, but for the most part we usually waited for it all to end to have the second staff meal of the day. These often took place at one in the morning, and sometimes they turned into late-night wine tastings, which was great, but wildly impractical, because at that time of day all the wine tasted equally good. We'd usually just have what deliciousness was left from the evening, but with a twist—and often that twist meant melted cheese.

CROQUE-MADAME

SERVES 4

This may be the most legendary sandwich in the world, at least in the eyes of the French: two slices of bread, ham, cheese, and a béchamel sauce topped with a fried egg. But calling it a sandwich tells only half the story; along with its cousin, the *croque-monsieur*, it's really a national dish, one that poets and artists have been feasting on in Parisian cafés for as long as these establishments have existed. Though neither a poet nor an artist, I like to keep the tradition alive. I have one ritual when I go to Paris: I head straight to Café de Flore in St Germain and order myself a *ballon de rouge* and a *croque-madame*. And at home I make sure my family is well steeped in this tradition, too, ready to carry it on for years to come. For ease and because I like the flavor, I use crème fraîche instead of béchamel, and this "sandwich" always turns out great. It's the perfect snack or meal, any time of day.

¾ POUND / 360 G GRUYÈRE CHEESE, GRATED (ABOUT 3 CUPS)

1 CUP / 90 G GRATED PARMESAN CHEESE

⅔ CUP / 160 ML CRÈME FRAÎCHE

1 TABLESPOON DIJON MUSTARD

2 LARGE EGG YOLKS

¼ TEASPOON GRATED NUTMEG

FINE SEA SALT AND FRESHLY GROUND BLACK PEPPER

2 TABLESPOONS / 30 G UNSALTED BUTTER, AT ROOM TEMPERATURE

8 SLICES WHITE SANDWICH BREAD

8 THICK SLICES HAM (¾ POUND / 340 G TOTAL)

1 TABLESPOON EXTRA-VIRGIN OLIVE OIL

4 LARGE EGGS

PINCH OF PIMENT D'ESPELETTE OR MILD CHILE POWDER

1. Preheat the oven to 400°F / 200°C. Line a baking sheet with parchment paper.

2. In a large bowl, mix together the Gruyère, Parmesan, crème fraîche, mustard, egg yolks, and nutmeg. Season with salt and pepper.

3. Butter each slice of bread and then turn them buttered side down. To 4 of the slices, add a layer of the cheese mixture, a slice of ham, another layer of cheese mixture, and a second piece of ham. You'll use up all of the ham and about two-thirds of the cheese mixture. Cover with a slice of bread, buttered side up, and spread the remaining cheese mixture on top. Season with black pepper.

4. Place the sandwiches on the lined baking sheet and transfer to the oven. Bake until golden brown and bubbling, about 15 minutes.

5. Meanwhile, in a sauté pan, heat the olive oil over medium-high heat. Carefully break each egg into it. When the white turns opaque and the edges are slightly golden, they're ready, about 3 minutes.

6. Put each *croque-madame* on a serving plate and top with an egg. Season each egg with salt, pepper, and piment d'Espelette. Serve immediately.

TOMATES FARÇIES

SERVES 6

We tend to have an overabundance of tomatoes in summer, and while my husband is very happy admiring them and photographing them, I feel they need to be put to use. About half end up in a gazpacho (page 72), but the rest are divided into salads, tomato sauces (some conserved for winter), various roasts, and casseroles. The really big ones sometimes get selected for a more prestigious task, that of being stuffed and roasted. It's not every tomato that can perform such a job: Applicants must be overwhelmingly tasty, yet sturdy enough to stand up to cooking. I like to use very flavorful sausage meat for the farce, and I find that adding ground hazelnuts on top adds a tasty little twist. This is a dish that can be prepared in advance and baked on command. These go very well with a glass of white Bordeaux, though my favorite pairing is a crisp rosé from Provence.

6 LARGE TOMATOES

2 SLICES STALE BREAD

⅓ CUP / 80 ML WHOLE MILK

6 PORK SAUSAGES, CASINGS REMOVED

2 SHALLOTS, FINELY CHOPPED

4 GARLIC CLOVES, MINCED

1 LARGE EGG

1 TABLESPOON DIJON MUSTARD

A LARGE HANDFUL OF FRESH FLAT-LEAF PARSLEY LEAVES, FINELY CHOPPED, PLUS MORE FOR SERVING (CHOPPED)

LEAVES FROM A FEW SPRIGS OF FRESH THYME

FINE SEA SALT AND FRESHLY GROUND BLACK PEPPER

1 CUP / 60 G FRESH BREAD CRUMBS

½ CUP / 60 G GROUND HAZELNUTS

5 TABLESPOONS / 75 ML EXTRA-VIRGIN OLIVE OIL

1. Preheat the oven to 400°F / 200°C.

2. Slice off the top part of each tomato to make a little "hat"; set aside. Gently scoop out the tomato pulp (reserve for another use) and arrange the tomatoes upside down on a plate to drain for 10 minutes.

3. Soak the bread in a bowl with the milk until softened, about 8 minutes.

4. Squeeze out the bread (discard the milk) and put it in a large bowl. Add the sausage meat, shallots, half of the garlic, the egg, mustard, parsley, and thyme and season with salt and pepper.

5. Turn the tomatoes over and sprinkle the bottoms of each with salt, pepper, and a teaspoon of bread crumbs. Fill the tomatoes with the sausage stuffing until full.

6. In a small bowl, combine the remaining bread crumbs, remaining garlic, and the ground hazelnuts. Sprinkle this mixture over the tomatoes.

7. Pour 2 tablespoons of the olive oil into a baking dish and add the stuffed tomatoes. Drizzle the remaining 3 tablespoons olive oil over the tomatoes and top them with the little hats. Bake until golden, about 40 minutes. Sprinkle with parsley and serve hot.

ENDIVES WITH HAM

⚡ SERVES 4 TO 6 ⚡

People often describe their food as comforting, but in this case I'd go one step further and call this grandmother fare—even more comforting than most comfort foods. And in grandmotherly style, it's also a great way to make children eat their vegetables. Wrap the endives in ham, cover them with a creamy béchamel sauce, and serve with freshly baked bread. Who could resist that? Certainly not the children who worked in my pop-up restaurant last summer. Behind the scenes, this admittedly wintery dish was one of the hits of the summer.

6 ENDIVES

3 TABLESPOONS / 45 G UNSALTED BUTTER

⅓ CUP / 40 G ALL-PURPOSE FLOUR

2 CUPS / 500 ML WHOLE MILK

¼ TEASPOON GRATED NUTMEG

FINE SEA SALT AND FRESHLY GROUND BLACK PEPPER

2 TABLESPOONS DIJON MUSTARD

6 SLICES HAM

1 CUP / 100 G GRATED GRUYÈRE OR EMMENTAL CHEESE

1. Preheat the oven to 350°F / 180°C.

2. Fill a large pot with an inch or two of water and bring to a boil over medium-high heat. Add a steamer insert to the pot, making sure the water does not touch the insert. Add the endives to the steamer and cover the pot with a lid. Steam until tender, about 15 minutes.

3. Meanwhile, in a medium saucepan, melt the butter over medium heat. Add the flour and whisk until smooth. Pour in the milk and whisk constantly until smooth. When the mixture starts to boil, reduce the heat and simmer until thick and creamy, about 10 minutes. Remove the béchamel from the heat and season with the nutmeg and salt and pepper.

4. Drain the endives head down—they retain a lot of water so it is important to drain as much as possible. I use paper towels and gently squeeze out excess water with my hands just to be sure. Spread a light layer of mustard on the endives and then roll each one in a slice of ham. Season lightly with salt and pepper.

5. Arrange the endives in a baking dish. Pour the béchamel sauce on top and sprinkle with the cheese. Bake until golden brown and bubbling, about 30 minutes.

EGGS PIPERADE

SERVES 4

I'm very fond of Basque cooking and love making piperade, which is kind of a Basque-style ratatouille that goes very well with fish, chicken, and, in this case, a simple fried egg. Sometimes, when I have an abundance of colorful peppers and tomatoes, I make several jars of piperade and keep them in the fridge. When there is no time to make something elaborate, and when the kids, or the restaurant staff, are too hungry and practically banging the silverware on the table, that's when the simplest, fastest dishes are needed. I pour a jar of piperade into a pan and make holes for the eggs, one per person. Sometimes I throw in a good chorizo sausage. It couldn't be simpler and it couldn't be tastier. This dish is also quite nice served as a decadent, savory breakfast or brunch—a Spanish alternative to bacon and eggs.

3 TABLESPOONS EXTRA-VIRGIN OLIVE OIL

1 TABLESPOON / 15 G UNSALTED BUTTER

2 MEDIUM YELLOW ONIONS, THINLY SLICED

2 RED BELL PEPPERS, CUT INTO THIN STRIPS

1 GREEN BELL PEPPER, CUT INTO THIN STRIPS

2 GARLIC CLOVES, THINLY SLICED

LEAVES FROM A FEW SPRIGS OF FRESH THYME

1 BAY LEAF

FINE SEA SALT AND FRESHLY GROUND BLACK PEPPER

2 TOMATOES, DICED

4 LARGE EGGS

4 THIN SLICES BAYONNE HAM OR PROSCIUTTO

PINCH OF PIMENT D'ESPELETTE OR MILD CHILE POWDER

1. Preheat the oven to 400°F / 200°C.

2. In a Dutch oven, heat the olive oil and butter over medium heat. Add the onions and sauté until softened, about 3 minutes. Add the bell peppers and continue to cook for 5 minutes. Stir in the garlic, thyme, and bay leaf and season with salt and black pepper. Cook for 1 minute. Add the tomatoes, stir gently, and cook until all of the vegetables are soft and fragrant, about 15 minutes. Discard the bay leaf.

3. Spoon the piperade into 4 individual ovenproof dishes, make a little well in the center, and break an egg into each. Drape a slice of ham over each serving. Bake until the egg whites are set but the yolks are still runny, 10 to 12 minutes.

4. Sprinkle piment d'Espelette and a little salt over each egg. Serve immediately.

HAM AND SPRING ONION OMELETTE

SERVES 1 TO 2

My husband is a pretty good cook, although he always denies it. He will whip up something from time to time when I ask him—or if he really wants a particular dish, often something gamey. But he has a ritual of making omelettes on Sunday mornings, and though he is exceedingly slow at it, we all love them. First the kitchen must be cleaned to hospital standards. Then he offers everyone a customized omelette, making them per person, one at a time. The kids all have their special requests: Some want no cheese, some want theirs extra spicy. Mia always wants everything, which results in what I can only think is a terrible omelette, but she disagrees and always finishes it. I have come to love this ham and spring onion combination with a sprinkle of basil and, though I am loath to admit it, I can't imagine Sundays without it—not least because it means I don't have to get out of bed.

1 TABLESPOON / 15 G UNSALTED BUTTER

½ TABLESPOON EXTRA-VIRGIN OLIVE OIL

2 SMALL SPRING ONIONS, WHITE AND GREEN PARTS, THINLY SLICED

3 LARGE EGGS

FINE SEA SALT AND FRESHLY GROUND BLACK PEPPER

2 THIN SLICES HAM, CUT INTO STRIPS

A HANDFUL OF CHOPPED FRESH BASIL

1 TABLESPOON GRATED CANTAL OR OTHER STRONG GRATING CHEESE

PINCH OF PIMENT D'ESPELETTE OR MILD CHILE POWDER

1. In a medium sauté pan, heat the butter and olive oil over medium heat. Add the spring onions and cook until golden, about 3 minutes.

2. Meanwhile, whisk the eggs with salt and pepper.

3. Add the eggs to the pan and cook over medium-high heat. When the eggs start to set in the center, add the ham, most of the basil, and the cheese. Just when the edges start to become slightly golden but the eggs are still a bit runny in the center, fold both sides into the center on top of each other and flip the omelette over. Cook for just 30 seconds and then flip it onto a plate.

4. Sprinkle with the piment d'Espelette and remaining basil. Serve immediately.

MIMOLETTE AND COMTÉ MAC AND CHEESE

⟡ SERVES 6 TO 8 ⟡

This section of the book turned out to be a who's who of comfort food—and it wouldn't be complete without the king of comfort foods: mac and cheese. As a kid in Hong Kong, I remember reading about this exciting dish and desperately wanting to try it. I also remember my disappointment when, having coaxed my mother or some nanny into buying a ready-made version, I realized that maybe it wasn't the best food in the world after all. But all that is relative. You reap as you sow. I still believe in the power of mac and cheese when it is done right. With just enough glorious, pungent cheese, it can still be, on a good day, the best food that a little girl ever dreamed existed.

4 TABLESPOONS / 60 G UNSALTED BUTTER, PLUS MORE FOR THE PAN

1 CUP FRESH BREAD CRUMBS

1 GARLIC CLOVE, HALVED

3 TABLESPOONS ALL-PURPOSE FLOUR

2½ CUPS / 600 ML WHOLE MILK

1 TABLESPOON DIJON MUSTARD

PINCH OF NUTMEG

PINCH OF PIMENT D'ESPELETTE OR MILD CHILE POWDER

FINE SEA SALT AND FRESHLY GROUND BLACK PEPPER

1 POUND / 500 G DRIED SMALL PENNE OR MACARONI PASTA

10 OUNCES / 300 G MIMOLETTE CHEESE, GRATED (ABOUT 2⅔ CUPS)

5 OUNCES / 150 G COMTÉ CHEESE, GRATED (ABOUT 1⅓ CUPS)

1. Preheat the oven to 350°F / 180°C. Butter a large ovenproof skillet.

2. Bring a large pot of salted water to a boil over medium-high heat.

3. In a food processor, pulse the bread crumbs with the garlic and 1 tablespoon / 15 g of the butter.

4. In a medium skillet, melt the remaining 3 tablespoons / 45 g butter over medium heat. Whisk in the flour. Immediately whisk in the milk, little by little, and simmer until the sauce thickens, about 2 minutes. Whisk in the mustard, nutmeg, and piment d'Espelette and season with salt and pepper.

5. Add the pasta to the boiling water and cook to al dente, according to the package directions.

6. Whisk half of each cheese into the sauce. When the pasta is al dente, drain and mix the pasta into the sauce in the pan until well combined, along with the rest of the grated cheese.

7. Pour the pasta mixture into the buttered ovenproof skillet. Scatter the bread-crumb mixture all over the dish and transfer to the oven. Bake until bubbling and golden brown, 30 to 35 minutes. Serve hot.

KALE AND SAUSAGE PASTA

~ SERVES 4 ~

Kale is a relative newcomer in French kitchens, so new that we don't really have a French name for it. We just call it *chou* (cabbage) *kale*—with a French accent, naturally. We started planting it in our vegetable garden about two years ago, not really having any specific idea of what to do with it. It has done us proud, a constant top performer that starts giving early and keeps on giving until Christmas. We use kale a lot in salads, which is delicious and healthy; I like to roast it in the oven and use it to garnish various dishes, like kale tartlets; and when we harvest too much of it, and we always do, I make this simple but highly appetizing pasta dish. Cooked kale is so different from raw, and with all the juices from the sausages, mixed with a healthy dose of Parmesan, this turns out to be a most satisfying dish.

½ CUP / 120 ML EXTRA-VIRGIN OLIVE OIL

14 OUNCES / 400 G PORK SAUSAGE, CASINGS REMOVED

1 SMALL RED ONION, THINLY SLICED

1¼ CUPS / 250 G CHOPPED KALE

FINE SEA SALT AND FRESHLY GROUND BLACK PEPPER

PINCH OF CRUSHED RED PEPPER FLAKES

1 POUND / 500 G DRIED RIGATONI

5 OUNCES / 120 G GRATED PARMESAN CHEESE (ABOUT 1⅓ CUPS), PLUS MORE FOR SERVING (OPTIONAL)

1. Bring a large pot of salted water to a boil over medium-high heat.

2. Meanwhile, in a large sauté pan, heat the olive oil over high heat. Add the sausage and cook, breaking it up with a wooden spoon, until well browned, about 5 minutes. Add the onion and continue to cook for 5 minutes. Add the kale, season with salt and black pepper, and cook and toss everything together for 3 minutes more. Sprinkle in the pepper flakes.

3. Add the pasta to the boiling water and cook to al dente, according to the package directions. Reserving ½ cup / 120 ml of the pasta water, drain the pasta and return it to the pot.

4. Add the sausage mixture, Parmesan, and reserved pasta water to the pasta, mix everything together, and serve immediately, topped with additional Parmesan, if desired.

WISE GUY CHICKEN

SERVES 4 TO 6

I love movies, especially old classics with cliché characters. The French guy playing the harmonica in the market on a Saturday. The blonde girl with the horrible American accent in a Godard movie or the greaser in the leather jacket who is so clearly destined for failure. And I have a particularly soft spot for wise guys who take time from their other work to cook up a little feast, the perfect tomato sauce, the best meatballs in the world. This is a simple dish I often make when I have no time to make anything. My kids love it and, despite the name, this may be the most honest crowd-pleaser of all. Who doesn't like chicken, especially when it is smothered in tomato sauce and melted cheese? This recipe is so easy to make, such a sure bet, that it almost feels like cheating—which is exactly why it deserves its name.

6 LARGE BONE-IN, SKIN-ON
CHICKEN BREASTS

3 TABLESPOONS EXTRA-VIRGIN
OLIVE OIL, PLUS MORE FOR
DRIZZLING

FINE SEA SALT AND FRESHLY
GROUND BLACK PEPPER

1 TEASPOON CHOPPED FRESH
ROSEMARY LEAVES

1 TEASPOON CHOPPED FRESH
THYME LEAVES

1½ CUPS / 360 ML MARINARA
SAUCE, HOMEMADE (PAGE 224) OR
STORE-BOUGHT

¾ CUP / 65 G GRATED MOZZARELLA
CHEESE

¾ CUP / 65 G GRATED PARMESAN
CHEESE

2 TABLESPOONS / 30 G UNSALTED
BUTTER, CUT INTO CUBES

1. Preheat the oven to 400°F / 200°C.

2. Drizzle the chicken breasts with olive oil and season with salt and pepper. Sprinkle the rosemary and thyme all over.

3. In a large skillet, heat the 3 tablespoons olive oil over medium-high heat. Add the chicken breasts and cook until slightly golden, about 5 minutes on each side.

4. Transfer the chicken to a baking dish, pour the marinara sauce all over, and scatter the mozzarella and Parmesan on top. Dot with the butter. Bake until bubbling and golden, about 15 minutes. Serve hot.

MARINARA SAUCE

⅓ CUP / 80 ML OLIVE OIL

1 MEDIUM ONION, DICED

3 GARLIC CLOVES, MINCED

2 CANS (14 OUNCES / 400 G EACH)
CHOPPED TOMATOES, DRAINED

½ CUP / 120 ML RED WINE

1 TABLESPOON TOMATO PASTE

1 TEASPOON DRIED OREGANO

A HANDFUL OF FRESH BASIL LEAVES,
CHOPPED

FINE SEA SALT AND FRESHLY
GROUND BLACK PEPPER

In a saucepan, heat the olive oil over medium-low heat. Add the onion and cook until tender, about 6 minutes. Add the garlic and cook for 2 minutes. Stir in the tomatoes, red wine, tomato paste, oregano, and basil. Season with salt and pepper. Instead of putting a lid on the pan, I cover the saucepan with a sheet of parchment paper cut to fit; I find this trick makes the sauce perfect in texture. Simmer over low heat until flavorful and thickened, about 30 minutes. Once cool, the sauce will keep covered in the refrigerator for up to a couple of weeks.

SIDE DISHES

BEET SALAD *with* **CRÈME FRAÎCHE** *233*

ENDIVE, ROQUEFORT, *and* **WALNUT SALAD** *234*

BRAISED LEEKS VINAIGRETTE *237*

ROAST EGGPLANT *with* **PINE NUTS**
and **RAISINS** *238*

SWISS CHARD GRATIN *243*

GRATIN DAUPHINOIS *244*

GARLIC POTATO CHIPS *247*

DAUPHINE POTATOES *248*

MASHED POTATOES *with* **FENNEL** *251*

AÏOLI SAUCE *with* **NEW POTATOES** *252*

CHESTNUT BREAD *257*

PAIN D'EPICES *258*

ABOUT A WEEK after we moved to St Yzans, sometime in early January, Oddur, Mia, and Þórir went out for a walk with some of our dogs. By then we had realized that though the house at No 1 rue de Loudenne was the home of our dreams, the setup wasn't equally dreamy for the army of primarily hunting dogs we had assembled. They were used to roaming the forests on their own, digging for moles and snakes and rats, tearing up any plants they felt like, chewing on anything they could find. A much smaller, manicured courtyard with rosebushes and olive trees and sensitive elderly ladies occasionally passing by was never going to be anything but a poor substitute. For a few days after our move it seemed that Oddur would never do anything else for the rest of his life other than walk the dogs.

On that particular day in January, he and the kids unexpectedly found at least a partial solution to the dog dilemma and in the process also paved the way for a fruitful summer. Just down the street from our house, about two hundred yards from our front door, they found a rusty gate and behind it a secret garden heavy with a mixture of unwanted shrubs and weeds and wonderful fruit trees. They ventured inside uninvited and discovered another garden behind the first one, complete with an old barn, a dilapidated woodshed, and a view of the vineyards.

When they returned they gushed about their find: This garden was apparently the answer to all of our problems, from where to let the dogs play, to where to have outside dinner, to where to plant vegetables, and even to where to put the swimming pool (not that we ever planned to build one). Nobody seemed to be using this land—but surely someone, somewhere, had to own it?

Had we not been new to St Yzans, the answer would have been immediately clear. A place like this could only ever belong to one man, Mr. Monopoly himself, the man who collects questionable property the way other people collect, well, dogs. Monsieur Teyssier seems to own half of St Yzans yet drives around in a beat-up little car, dresses simply, and arrives without much fanfare. Someone described him perfectly as the ideal spy, a man who can fit in anywhere and whom no one really

notices. Through Mr. Ladra, who sold us the house, we tracked down Mr. Teyssier, and he took the whole family on a tour of the secret garden. He wouldn't sell us the land (he never really sells anything), but he could see the benefit of our using it, for a small fee, especially if we put some order to the place. Regarding the fruit trees he would appreciate if he could still have some access to them: Perhaps some participation program could be arranged? In the end, an invisible contract was written and signed: We would take care of the place and manage it, and he could still enjoy it from time to time.

In March we fixed the old fences and built new ones. We fought and won our battle with the thorn forest and its allies, the stinging nettles and weeds. We decided where to build our vegetable garden, and Tim, our then resident gardener and musician from Cambridge, prepared the soil, and his girlfriend, Annie, sowed the seeds that would later become the foundation of our very successful summer garden. We planted the fava beans late—too late, in fact, so that our entire crop consisted of a handful of mediocre beans. But we had great success with the zucchini, whose flowers gave us great joy in May and early June. The Swiss chard had a part to play, as did the lettuces, radishes, and a couple of rows of spring onions. Thanks to my husband's impatience, the tomato seedlings went into the ground so early that Monsieur Teyssier thought we were mad (a continuing trend throughout the summer), but by mid-July we had our first crates of glorious tomatoes. The kale, which is rather a novelty in French cuisine and gardens, was one of the success stories of the summer: It grew with unabashed arrogance, taller than anyone could ever have expected, almost as tall as Gunnhildur, who took over the garden with aplomb when Tim returned to the UK. When I would walk by with our younger kids, I would sometimes see Monsieur Teyssier giving her a lecture on how to plant leeks or how to maintain tomato plants—or how to conjugate an irregular verb. Gunnsy's French grammar blossomed as much as the garden did that summer.

BEET SALAD WITH CRÈME FRAÎCHE

SERVES 4 TO 6

If this salad were a fairy tale, and it's certainly exciting enough to be one, it would go something like this: One day, when all the red vegetables had gotten tired of reading about how healthy and delicious their leafy green colleagues were, they got together and decided to do something about it. "I think, if we all pitch in, we could make a smashing salad," said the beet. "I agree," said the red onion. But they decided they needed a little help. So they sent the red cabbage to recruit the pomegranate. He was in: "I feel it is my duty to help you even if I like to work alone." The pumpkin seeds soon followed suit. A dollop of cream and some capers for contrast and they all headed to the big salad fair where they jumped into a bowl.

To put it simply, I can't think of a more delicious, beautiful, and healthy salad. I love making it, I love eating it, and afterward I always feel rejuvenated and happy. One note: Be sure to wear an apron when you seed the pomegranate; those red little guys are very juicy and lively.

2 MEDIUM BEETS, PEELED AND VERY THINLY SLICED

½ LARGE HEAD RED CABBAGE, CORED AND VERY THINLY SLICED

3 RED ENDIVES OR 2 SMALL TREVISO RADICCHIO, LEAVES SEPARATED

1 LARGE RED ONION, THINLY SLICED

SEEDS FROM 1 LARGE POMEGRANATE

½ CUP / 60 G PUMPKIN SEEDS, LIGHTLY TOASTED

LEAVES FROM A FEW SPRIGS OF FRESH FLAT-LEAF PARSLEY, FINELY CHOPPED

1 TABLESPOON DRAINED CAPERS

3 TABLESPOONS EXTRA-VIRGIN OLIVE OIL

GRATED ZEST AND JUICE OF 1 LEMON

FINE SEA SALT AND FRESHLY GROUND BLACK PEPPER

½ CUP / 120 ML CRÈME FRAÎCHE

1. In a medium bowl, combine the beets, cabbage, endives, onion, pomegranate seeds, pumpkin seeds, parsley, and capers.

2. In a small bowl, whisk together the olive oil and lemon juice and season with salt and pepper. Drizzle over the salad and toss everything together.

3. Serve the salad on plates, topping it with the crème fraîche and lemon zest.

ENDIVE, ROQUEFORT, AND WALNUT SALAD

I am very fond of perfect pairings, often simple ones you might not necessarily think of until one day you do. Like the moment someone tries port wine with Roquefort for the first time, or dips Parmesan cheese into balsamic vinegar, or sprinkles toast with rosemary and salt before dipping it into a soft-boiled egg. This salad, a long-standing favorite of mine, would easily fall into this category. It's a pairing thing, more an introduction of ingredients than an alchemy of cooking: crunchy, bitter, sweet, nutty, creamy, and tangy all at once. When I have this salad I like to splurge on a really good white Burgundy or even, dare I say it, a top-notch California Chardonnay.

3 ENDIVES, QUARTERED
LENGTHWISE AND CORED

2 SMALL APPLES, THINLY SLICED

10 WALNUTS

3 TABLESPOONS WALNUT OIL

1 TEASPOON GRATED LEMON ZEST

1 TABLESPOON FRESH LEMON JUICE

FLEUR DE SEL AND FRESHLY
GROUND BLACK PEPPER

4 OUNCES / 110 G ROQUEFORT OR
BLEU D'AUVERGNE CHEESE

In a large salad bowl, toss together the endives, apples, and walnuts. Drizzle the walnut oil on top and add the lemon zest and juice. Season with fleur de sel and pepper. Finally, crumble the cheese on top and mix together gently. Serve immediately.

BRAISED LEEKS VINAIGRETTE

～ SERVES 4 TO 6 ～

In my kitchen, next to the stove, there is a small pantry corner, just a windowsill, really, and it's always filled with fresh vegetables. In the middle there is a copper pot filled with onions, and to the left of it a stack of potatoes. On the right side we always have a bundle of carrots and one row of fresh leeks. In front of the carrots we usually have a mix of what's in season, say zucchini and eggplant. All this is my husband's doing; I don't really arrange vegetables as if they were a still life, but he does. He is from Iceland, where people have a history of believing in elves, but he's also a realist, so he knows that things don't really happen by themselves. So he is happy to play the vegetable elf. When he senses that some vegetables are peaking and need to be cooked, he will simply take them out and place them in the middle of the kitchen. When that vegetable is leeks, I braise them to serve as a side dish or a starter—for there aren't many recipes that require a dozen leeks. This is French cooking, not at its most extravagant but certainly at its purest and best.

FOR THE LEEKS

8 MEDIUM LEEKS

2 TABLESPOONS EXTRA-VIRGIN
OLIVE OIL

2 GARLIC CLOVES, THINLY SLICED

FINE SEA SALT AND FRESHLY
GROUND BLACK PEPPER

3 TABLESPOONS WHITE WINE

¼ CUP / 60 ML CHICKEN OR
VEGETABLE STOCK

FOR THE VINAIGRETTE

⅓ CUP / 80 ML EXTRA-VIRGIN
OLIVE OIL

1 TABLESPOON DIJON MUSTARD

2 TABLESPOONS SHERRY VINEGAR

FINE SEA SALT AND FRESHLY
GROUND BLACK PEPPER

SMALL HANDFUL OF FRESH CHIVES,
FINELY CHOPPED

1. **PREPARE THE LEEKS.** Trim the dark green tops of the leeks and the roots and remove the outer layer from each one. Rinse each leek under cold running water.

2. In a large pot, heat the olive oil over medium heat. Add the garlic and cook for a minute. Add the leeks, season with salt and pepper, and cook for 5 minutes. Pour in the wine and simmer for 2 minutes to reduce. Pour in the stock. Cover and cook until the leeks are tender but not overly soft, about 10 minutes.

3. **MEANWHILE, MAKE THE VINAIGRETTE.** In a small bowl, whisk together the olive oil, mustard, and vinegar. Season with salt and pepper.

4. Halve the leeks and put them in a serving dish. Drizzle the vinaigrette over them and sprinkle the chives on top.

ROAST EGGPLANT WITH
PINE NUTS AND RAISINS

⟿ SERVES 6 ⟿

I have to admit that I'm stepping over the border to Italy with this recipe, but it's so good and simple that I had to include it. It landed in this book by pure coincidence, brought on by the fact that I went on holiday in Umbria in the middle of an eggplant inundation, courtesy of our vegetable garden. I had tried to keep up, but for every eggplant I cooked, three more appeared. You don't need so many for ratatouille, and the family was quite frankly getting fed up with baba ghanoush. When we returned to St Yzans, I had a head full of ideas for tackling the eggplant, and this one—perfect as a side dish with meat—is the one I fell in love with most.

⅓ CUP / 80 ML EXTRA-VIRGIN OLIVE
OIL, PLUS MORE FOR DRIZZLING

2 LARGE EGGPLANTS, SLICED
½ INCH / 1.5 CM THICK

FINE SEA SALT AND FRESHLY
GROUND BLACK PEPPER

A HANDFUL OF PINE NUTS

A HANDFUL OF RAISINS

1. Preheat the oven to 400°F / 200°C. Line 2 baking sheets with parchment paper.

2. In a large sauté pan, heat the olive oil over medium-high heat. Working in batches, cook the eggplant slices until nicely browned, about 2 minutes on each side. Season with salt and pepper.

3. Arrange the eggplant slices in a single layer on the baking sheets and scatter the pine nuts and raisins on top. Drizzle a little bit of olive oil over everything and transfer to the oven. Roast until the eggplant is golden, about 10 minutes. Serve immediately.

SWISS CHARD GRATIN

～ SERVES 4 ～

I have a penchant for dark green, leafy vegetables such as kale, spinach, and Swiss chard. They are versatile, delicious, and, if reports are to be believed, just about the healthiest food we can consume. As a child living in Asia, I ate various greens, often stir-fried in a pan with oil and garlic. That's still one of the most delightful ways to enjoy them, but these days I include them in all sorts of dishes: cakes and tarts and quiches, scrambled eggs and omelettes, and fresh salads as a side dish with meat or fish. This chard gratin is a wonderful alternative to serving potatoes with a meal and yet another way to help children grow up loving eating greens.

2 POUNDS / 900 G SWISS CHARD

2 TABLESPOONS EXTRA-VIRGIN OLIVE OIL

1 LARGE YELLOW ONION, THINLY SLICED

FINE SEA SALT AND FRESHLY GROUND BLACK PEPPER

2 TABLESPOONS / 30 G UNSALTED BUTTER

2½ TABLESPOONS ALL-PURPOSE FLOUR

1 CUP / 240 ML WHOLE MILK

PINCH OF GRATED NUTMEG

1 CUP / 90 G GRATED GRUYÈRE CHEESE

1. Preheat the oven to 400F° / 200°C.

2. Chop the Swiss chard leaves coarsely and slice the stems into 2-inch / 5 cm pieces.

3. In a large sauté pan, heat the olive oil over medium-high heat. Add the onion and cook until translucent, about 3 minutes. Add the chard, season with salt and pepper, and cook for 10 minutes over medium-low heat. Transfer the mixture to a 12-inch / 30 cm oval baking dish.

4. In a small saucepan, melt the butter over medium heat. Whisk in the flour until smooth. Whisk in the milk and cook, whisking, until the mixture starts to boil. Reduce the heat and simmer until thick and creamy, about 10 minutes. Season the béchamel sauce with the nutmeg and salt and pepper.

5. Pour the béchamel over the chard in the baking dish, scatter the Gruyère on top, and bake until bubbling and golden brown, about 25 minutes. Serve immediately.

GRATIN DAUPHINOIS

⟿ SERVES 6 ⟿

A side dish is like a supporting actor. It needs to be good, it can't spoil the show, and the rest of the cast relies on it—but whatever happens it will never be the star of the show. By that definition, *gratin dauphinois* isn't a side dish. When I make it, which is often, I usually build my meal around it. I start just knowing I want *gratin dauphinois*, so incredibly rewarding—which is surprising for a potato dish that is so subtle and mild. Then I start thinking of a meat to serve with it, almost as an afterthought. Imagine a character actor who bursts onto stage, steals the audience, and gets away with it. That's *gratin dauphinois*.

2 POUNDS / 900 G YUKON GOLD
POTATOES

2 CUPS / 480 ML HEAVY CREAM

1 CUP / 240 ML WHOLE MILK

1 TEASPOON GRATED NUTMEG

FINE SEA SALT AND FRESHLY
GROUND BLACK PEPPER

3 GARLIC CLOVES

1 TABLESPOON / 15 G UNSALTED
BUTTER

1. Preheat the oven to 350°F / 180°C.

2. Peel and slice the potatoes into thin slices, each about ⅛ inch / 3 mm thick. I use my food processor or a mandoline for this.

3. In a very large saucepan, combine the cream and milk. Season with the nutmeg and salt and pepper and whisk everything together. Put the saucepan over medium heat and bring the mixture to a low boil. Add the potato slices, reduce the heat, and simmer for 10 minutes.

4. Meanwhile, thinly slice the garlic and rub a few slices over the bottom of a 9-inch / 23 cm round baking dish. Rub a little of the butter all over.

5. Using a slotted spoon, layer the potato slices into the dish, adding a few slices of garlic here and there. Pour the milk mixture all over and season with salt and pepper. Scatter the remaining butter on top.

6. Bake until golden brown and bubbling, 30 to 40 minutes. Serve immediately.

GARLIC POTATO CHIPS

⌾ SERVES 4 ⌾

I love trying out restaurants I haven't been to before, especially old bistros that have somehow escaped me. But this can be risky business. What if, forgetting for a moment the gorgeous zinc bar and the pretty Champagne glasses, the food simply isn't any good? The menu often offers little help, all the classics nicely arranged in a beautiful typeface. But they can be great or disastrous, depending on how they're made. So I look around me, trying to see what people are having, searching for clues. And then it happens. A waiter in black pants and a long white apron brings out a huge serving dish, filled with the crispiest, most delicious-looking potato chips you'll ever see. That's when I know everything is going to be fine. A place that serves potatoes like that isn't going to mess up the rest of it—and even if they do, having these potatoes makes the whole meal worthwhile.

1 POUND / 450 G RUSSET POTATOES

2 CUPS / 475 ML RENDERED
DUCK FAT

FLEUR DE SEL

3 GARLIC CLOVES, THINLY SLICED

1. Peel the potatoes, then slice them as thinly as possible with a mandoline. Soak the potatoes in a bowl of cold water for 3 minutes. Drain and pat dry. Wrap in a clean kitchen towel and set aside.

2. In a large pot, heat the duck fat over medium heat to 325°F / 160°C. Test the temperature of the duck fat by dropping in a small piece of potato. If the potato turns golden within seconds, the oil is ready. Working in batches, fry the potato slices, turning once, until golden and crisp, 2 to 3 minutes. Remove with a slotted spoon, drain on paper towels, and season with fleur de sel.

3. Fry the garlic slices for a minute (they cook very quickly) and scatter all over the chips. Serve immediately.

DAUPHINE POTATOES

~~~ SERVES 4 TO 6 ~~~

The road to a better book is paved with small victories and embarrassing defeats. It's a journey I've been on for quite a few years now, and though they say that you learn nothing from winning, that all the wisdom comes from losing, I must say I much prefer success in the kitchen than a hard-learned lesson. One of my first significant victories came many years ago with Dauphine potatoes. I had had them all my life, with a Sunday steak in restaurants or at my grandmother's in the South of France, but I never thought I would ever make these puffed-up little beauties myself. Then one morning, as a student in Paris, I woke up and just decided to give it a go. They turned out perfectly, and I've been making them ever since. I love to serve them when I have a dinner party and the menu is a bit old-fashioned. They are ideal for glamorously scooping up thick, red wine sauce.

1 POUND / 450 G RUSSET POTATOES, PEELED AND DICED

7 TABLESPOONS / 100 G UNSALTED BUTTER

¼ TEASPOON GRATED NUTMEG

PINCH OF FINE SEA SALT, PLUS MORE FOR SEASONING

1⅔ CUPS / 200 G ALL-PURPOSE FLOUR, PLUS MORE FOR DREDGING

4 LARGE EGGS

VEGETABLE OIL, FOR DEEP-FRYING

1. Pour an inch or two of water into a large pot and bring to a boil over medium-high heat. Add a steamer insert to the pot, making sure the water does not touch the insert. Add the potatoes to the steamer, cover, and steam until tender, about 15 minutes.

2. Meanwhile, prepare the choux dough. In a large saucepan, combine ¾ cup / 180 ml water with the butter, nutmeg, and salt. Bring to a low boil over medium heat. Remove from the heat, add the flour, and mix well with a wooden spoon. Add the eggs, one at a time, mixing well between additions until you get a smooth dough. Return the saucepan to the stove and stir briskly for a minute over medium heat to dry out the dough. Remove from the heat.

3. Drain the potatoes and, while they are still hot, mash them as finely as possible in a bowl. Add the potatoes to the choux dough and mix together.

4. In a large pot, heat about 2 inches / 5 cm of vegetable oil over medium heat to 325°F / 160°C. Test the temperature of the oil by dropping in a small piece of dough. If the dough turns golden within seconds, the oil is ready. Shape the dough with your hands into small balls, each about the size of a golf ball. Dredge in flour, shaking off the excess. Working in batches, fry the balls in the oil until golden brown, about 8 minutes, turning once. Remove with a slotted spoon, drain on paper towels, and season with salt. Let cool for 5 minutes before serving.

MASHED POTATOES WITH FENNEL

SERVES 4

We all love a good purée, and frankly I find it hard to get bored with simple, well-made mashed potatoes. Sometimes I add a bit of cheese, sometimes garlic. From time to time I change things up: I make cauliflower purée or, in autumn, a pumpkin purée. But I always come back to potatoes. I have gotten into the habit of serving grilled pork with this version, which adds fragrant fennel to the mix for an alluring side dish that plays nicely with smoky meat.

1 POUND / 450 G RUSSET POTATOES, PEELED AND DICED

1 FENNEL BULB, DICED (RESERVE THE LEAFY FRONDS FOR GARNISH)

3 TABLESPOONS HEAVY CREAM

2 TABLESPOONS / 30 G UNSALTED BUTTER

1 LARGE EGG YOLK

FINE SEA SALT AND FRESHLY GROUND BLACK PEPPER

1. Pour an inch or two of water into a large pot and bring to a boil over medium-high heat. Add a steamer insert to the pot, making sure the water does not touch the insert. Add the potatoes and fennel to the steamer, cover, and steam until tender, about 15 minutes.

2. Transfer the vegetables to a warm serving bowl and mash with a vegetable masher. Mix in the cream, butter, and egg yolk and season with salt and pepper. Serve garnished with the fennel fronds.

AÏOLI SAUCE WITH NEW POTATOES

SERVES 4

I grew up in Hong Kong with a Chinese father who loved food and a French mother who didn't love to cook, to say the least. As a result, a lot of my life was spent in restaurants, often Chinese but sometimes fancy French ones, which were the only type of French restaurants to be found in HK in those days. That's where I'd have my dose of duck confit, escargots, panfried veal liver, and all the rest of the classics.

Though my mother seldom ventured into the kitchen, she would get homesick for the south of France from time to time. I know it probably sounds selfish, but her being homesick made me incredibly happy, because that's when she'd put on her apron and make her favorite sauce, aïoli. She never said anything, but I would see her in the kitchen chopping garlic, whisking eggs, and boiling new potatoes to dip in the sauce. Those are some of my favorite childhood memories. My father would soon catch wind of the sauce making and bring home big bags of fresh shrimp to share the sauce with the potatoes.

Now that I live in France I make this sauce quite regularly, often because I have made meringues and need something to do with the yolks. I add a little saffron, a small touch that I find enhances the sauce, especially when served with fresh seafood. And when I get homesick for my mother, I boil a few potatoes, too.

1 TEASPOON DIJON MUSTARD

1 TABLESPOON FRESH LEMON JUICE

1 LARGE EGG YOLK

FINE SEA SALT AND FRESHLY GROUND BLACK PEPPER

½ CUP / 120 ML VEGETABLE OIL

⅔ CUP / 160 ML EXTRA-VIRGIN OLIVE OIL

2 GARLIC CLOVES, MINCED

¼ TEASPOON SAFFRON THREADS, SOAKED IN A FEW DROPS OF LUKEWARM WATER

1 POUND / 450 G SMALL NEW POTATOES

LEAVES FROM 3 SPRIGS OF FRESH FLAT-LEAF PARSLEY

1. In a medium bowl, whisk together the mustard, lemon juice, egg yolk, and ½ teaspoon salt. Gradually drizzle in the vegetable and olive oils, whisking constantly. Add the garlic and saffron threads and continue to whisk until thick and creamy. Season with salt and pepper.

2. Pour an inch or two of water into a large pot and bring to a boil over medium-high heat. Add a steamer insert to the pot, making sure the water does not touch the insert. Add the potatoes to the steamer, cover, and steam until tender, about 15 minutes.

3. Season the potatoes lightly with salt and sprinkle with the parsley. Serve with the aïoli sauce for dipping.

CHESTNUT BREAD

MAKES 2 (9 × 5-INCH / 23 × 13 CM) LOAVES

Imagine this: A friend invites you over for lunch on a rainy Monday and says he's serving "soup and bread." Doesn't sound that exciting, does it? But the soup is a slightly spicy, slightly sweet pumpkin one made with homemade chicken stock. And the bread is a freshly baked chestnut loaf, still hot enough for the salty butter from Normandy to melt into the slices and for some of it to drip into the soup when you dip the bread in it. I almost forgot: The meal is served by a fire with a glass of very dry, slightly perfumed white Bordeaux. Now that is something special, especially the bread, which I can't stop dreaming about!

2 ENVELOPES (¼ OUNCE / 7 G EACH) ACTIVE DRY YEAST

3½ CUPS / 830 ML LUKEWARM WATER

5½ CUPS / 650 G ALL-PURPOSE FLOUR, PLUS MORE FOR THE BOWL

1 CUP / 120 G CHESTNUT FLOUR

7 OUNCES / 190 G PEELED COOKED CHESTNUTS (BOTTLED OR VACUUM-PACKED), FINELY CHOPPED

1 TABLESPOON FINE SEA SALT

1 TABLESPOON HONEY

UNSALTED BUTTER

1. Dissolve the yeast in 2 cups / 470 ml of the warm water. Let stand for 20 minutes.

2. In a large bowl, combine the two flours, the chestnuts, and salt. Make a well in the center and add the yeast mixture and honey. Start kneading, adding 1 more cup / 240 ml of the warm water. Keep kneading, adding the final ½ cup / 120 ml warm water as needed to make a sticky dough. Put the dough in a floured bowl, cover with a damp towel, and let it rise in a warm place until doubled in volume, 2 to 3 hours.

3. Preheat the oven to 350°F / 180°C. Grease 2 (9 × 5-inch / 23 × 13 cm) loaf pans.

4. Stir the dough to deflate. Divide the dough in half and pour into the prepared pans, filling each pan about three-quarters full. Cover the pans with clean kitchen towels and let the dough rise for another 30 minutes.

5. Bake until risen with a golden crust, about 40 minutes. Unmold the breads and let cool completely on a wire rack before serving.

PAIN D'EPICES

I have this ongoing debate in my head whether spice bread is sweet or savory—not that it really *needs* to be classified; I think it's perfectly happy swinging both ways. Still, the question lingers: What's the best way to serve it? When it is fresh out of the oven, I love to slice it thick, butter it generously, and enjoy it on its own, maybe with a cup of tea. I like it topped with a generous slice of foie gras, sprinkled with coarse sea salt, and served with a glass of well-chilled Sauternes. Other times I simply drench it in honey and have it with a glass of rosé Champagne. The next day, for breakfast I have it with homemade jam and a big cup of coffee. I feel like a rule is forming here: When spice bread is young, it's savory; when it ages it becomes more suitable for sweet. How do you like it best?

5½ TABLESPOONS / 80 G UNSALTED BUTTER, MELTED, PLUS MORE FOR THE PAN

1 CUP / 120 G ALL-PURPOSE FLOUR

¼ CUP / 30 G BUCKWHEAT FLOUR

⅓ CUP / 50 G ALMONDS, FINELY CHOPPED

2 TEASPOONS BAKING POWDER

¼ TEASPOON GROUND CINNAMON

¼ TEASPOON GRATED NUTMEG

¼ TEASPOON GROUND CLOVES

¼ TEASPOON GROUND GINGER

⅔ CUP / 160 ML LAVENDER HONEY

1 LARGE EGG YOLK

1. Preheat the oven to 350°F / 180°C. Grease a 9 × 5-inch / 23 × 13 cm loaf pan with butter.

2. In a large bowl, combine the flours, almonds, baking powder, cinnamon, nutmeg, cloves, and ginger. Add the honey, melted butter, and egg yolk and mix well.

3. Scrape the dough into the prepared pan and bake until a knife inserted in the center comes out clean, about 40 minutes.

4. Unmold and let cool at least slightly before serving. This is also good at room temperature.

DESSERTS

VANILLA RICE PUDDING *with* **SALTED BUTTER CARAMEL SAUCE** *264*

FRESH FIG TART *with* **HONEY** *and* **ORANGE FLOWER WATER** *267*

MY GRANDMOTHER'S CRÈME CARAMEL *271*

SALTED BUTTER CHOCOLATE CAKE *272*

WALNUT CAKE *276*

PLUM PAIN PERDU *279*

BABA AU RHUM *284*

BAKED APPLES *with* SPÉCULOOS *289*

STRAWBERRY TART *290*

RASPBERRY SOUFFLÉ *294*

CHERRY STEW *297*

ORANGE BLOSSOM CAKE *298*

BAKED PEARS *with* CHOCOLATE *301*

ROASTED PEACHES *with* PISTACHIO CREAM *302*

CHERRY *and* ALMOND CAKE *305*

ALMOND ICE CREAM *306*

PRUNE PARCELS *309*

WALNUT TART *310*

CRÊPES SUZETTE *312*

CHOCOLATE ICE CREAM *315*

VANILLA MARSHMALLOWS *316*

ALMOND TUILES *319*

MERVEILLEUX *320*

THERE IS FOOD and there is dessert. Food we have because we must, because we have to. It's often delicious, but ultimately we can't live without it. Desserts we have only because we want to. It sets them apart, makes their lives easy. Which is why I never worry about them. People send back under- or overcooked meat. They send back wine. But does anyone ever send back dessert? I don't think so. A waiter brings a dessert to your table. You taste it. You thought the soufflé would be softer inside and you discuss this with your tablemates. Then you take another spoonful. It's still pretty good. Then another. When the waiter finally comes back to your table the soufflé is gone—that's the only bad thing about it. He asks if he can get anything else for you. You think for a minute: Would it be possible to have another soufflé, please?

I know I am exaggerating slightly—there are certainly bad desserts—but by that time in the meal, if the dessert is any good at all, people tend to be more forgiving. They've had good food, they've had wine, and by now they've mostly made up their minds about how they'd rate the experience. A great dessert can lift it, and while a terrible one can sour it slightly, it won't make them leave; after all, they are leaving anyway.

I see this as a challenge. In life you can do just enough, or you can do a little bit more, give a little extra—even when it's not necessarily needed. You can, as they say, kill it.

Dessert is where I kill it.

VANILLA RICE PUDDING
WITH SALTED BUTTER CARAMEL SAUCE

SERVES 8

Rice pudding can be found in many cultures, perhaps because it is such a comforting dessert and the ingredients are usually already on hand. I like to use risotto rice, and I don't hold back on the vanilla and lemon zest. My kids love it topped with a thick, homemade, salted butter caramel. Sometimes I suspect that it's the caramel and not the pudding that they're really after, and if I weren't vigilant, I think they'd serve themselves a portion of half caramel. If I am being honest, I also have a tendency to go heavy on the caramel when no one is looking.

FOR THE RICE PUDDING

1 QUART / 1 LITER WHOLE MILK

¾ CUP / 150 G SUGAR

1 VANILLA BEAN, SPLIT LENGTHWISE, SEEDS SCRAPED AND RESERVED

GRATED ZEST OF 1 LEMON

1 CUP / 190 G ARBORIO RICE

1½ CUPS / 350 ML HEAVY CREAM

FOR THE CARAMEL SAUCE

¾ CUP / 150 G SUGAR

⅓ CUP PLUS 1 TABLESPOON / 95 ML HEAVY CREAM, SLIGHTLY WARM

2 TABLESPOONS / 30 G SALTED BUTTER

PINCH OF FLEUR DE SEL

1. **MAKE THE RICE PUDDING.** In a large saucepan, combine the milk, sugar, vanilla bean and seeds, and lemon zest. Stir over medium heat and bring to a simmer. Add the rice, reduce the heat to as low as possible, and cover with a lid. Simmer, stirring occasionally, until the rice is tender, about 40 minutes. Set aside to cool. Transfer to a bowl, cover with plastic wrap, and refrigerate until cold, at least 3 hours or overnight.

2. **MAKE THE CARAMEL SAUCE.** In a medium saucepan, heat the sugar over medium heat until it melts and turns amber colored. Remove the saucepan from the heat and carefully add the warm cream and the butter. Stir constantly with a spatula until smooth. Stir in the fleur de sel. Pour the caramel into a glass jar and let cool.

3. Whisk the heavy cream until it holds stiff peaks and then gently fold it into the rice pudding. Serve drizzled with the salted butter caramel sauce.

FRESH FIG TART WITH HONEY AND ORANGE FLOWER WATER

Figs are very near the top of my fruit list. Luckily, Médoc is filled with fig trees, and though we have none of our own, we have plenty of friends and neighbors who let us share in their bounty. I always bring a basket filled with little treats, because you can't really plunder someone's fig tree without offering some compensation, no matter how nice and hospitable they are. Sometimes I arrive with a little jar of homemade marmalade or jam, maybe a plum compote from our plum tree that came into season weeks earlier. Sometimes I bring a bottle of wine. But my favorite thing to bring is some puff pastry that I can roll out in seconds and then top with cream and the figs we just picked. This usually happens in late August or September, when it's still warm enough to have a picnic under the fig tree. These are the Sundays I dream of in winter.

8 OUNCES / 230 G FROZEN PUFF PASTRY, THAWED

1 CUP / 250 ML HEAVY CREAM

⅓ CUP / 80 ML MASCARPONE CHEESE

4 TO 5 TABLESPOONS HONEY (TO TASTE), PLUS MORE FOR DRIZZLING

1 VANILLA BEAN, SPLIT LENGTHWISE, SEEDS SCRAPED AND RESERVED

5 TABLESPOONS / 75 ML ORANGE FLOWER WATER

10 FRESH FIGS, QUARTERED

¼ CUP / 40 G SLICED ALMONDS, LIGHTLY TOASTED

1. Preheat the oven to 400°F / 200°C. Line a baking sheet with parchment paper.

2. Roll out the pastry lightly into a rectangular shape and fold in a ¾-inch / 2 cm border on all sides. Transfer to the lined baking sheet. Prick the pastry all over with a fork. Top with a second sheet of parchment paper and pie weights or a second baking sheet. Bake until the pastry is golden, about 15 minutes. Set aside to cool.

3. In a large bowl, combine the heavy cream, mascarpone, honey, and vanilla bean seeds. Whisk the mixture until it starts to thicken, then add the orange flower water. Whisk until the cream is thick and easy to spread.

4. When the pastry is cool, spread the cream all over and arrange the quartered figs on top. Scatter the almonds on top and drizzle honey all over. Serve within 1 hour.

MY GRANDMOTHER'S CRÈME CARAMEL

Crème brûlée is just as iconic and equally famous in the world of French sweets, but there is something distinctly more old-fashioned about crème caramel. I will always associate this dessert with my sweet little grandmother Séraphine, who made it every Sunday in the South of France. This is her recipe, which I've made again and again until I figured out any pitfalls and perfected it. Now I can make crème caramel that does justice to my grandmother, and so can you.

FOR THE CARAMEL

1 CUP / 200 G SUGAR

½ TABLESPOON UNSALTED BUTTER

FOR THE CUSTARD

1 CUP / 240 ML HEAVY CREAM

1 CUP / 240 ML WHOLE MILK

1 VANILLA BEAN, SPLIT LENGTHWISE, SEEDS SCRAPED AND RESERVED

1 TEASPOON GRATED LEMON ZEST

PINCH OF FINE SEA SALT

4 LARGE EGGS

¼ CUP / 50 G SUGAR

1. Have ready an 8-inch / 20 cm fluted brioche mold or other decorative ovenproof mold.

2. **MAKE THE CARAMEL.** In a medium saucepan, melt the sugar over medium heat without stirring. Once the sugar has dissolved, boil until the color turns uniformly dark amber. Remove immediately from the heat and carefully pour it into the mold. Swirl the mold in a circular motion so the caramel coats the entire bottom. Once the caramel is cool, butter the sides of the ramekin (this will facilitate the unmolding later).

3. Preheat the oven to 300°F / 150°C. Bring a kettle of water to a boil.

4. **MAKE THE CUSTARD.** In a large saucepan, combine the cream, milk, vanilla bean and seeds, lemon zest, and salt over medium heat until hot but not boiling.

5. In a large bowl, whisk together the eggs and sugar until pale and fluffy. When the milk is hot but not boiling, discard the vanilla pod and slowly whisk the liquid into the egg mixture. Gently pour into the mold.

6. Set the mold in a roasting pan or deep baking dish. Gently pour boiling water into the roasting pan to come halfway up the sides of the mold. Carefully transfer to the oven and bake until the custard is set in the center, about 50 minutes. Remove from the water bath and let cool completely. Refrigerate for at least 1 hour, until cooled.

7. To serve, gently loosen the sides of the custard with a butter knife. Invert a rimmed serving dish (make sure it is deep enough to hold the caramel sauce) on top and gently turn everything upside down. Remove the mold. Serve each portion with a few spoons of caramel sauce.

SALTED BUTTER CHOCOLATE CAKE

SERVES 6

This is the dessert I make when I don't know what dessert to make. It sounds like a second choice, but it's not at all. It's the popular choice, the one that I know everybody will always like and that never goes out of fashion. The salted butter is a subtle touch; you can taste it, but I'm careful never to let it overpower the chocolate, which would be hard anyway, because this cake is just so chocolate-y. I like to bake this cake so it's set but still moist, but my kids often ask me to take it out a minute or two earlier so it's runny and delicious. The choice is yours.

6½ TABLESPOONS / 90 G SALTED BUTTER, PLUS MORE FOR THE PAN

8 OUNCES / 230 G BITTERSWEET CHOCOLATE, CHOPPED

6 LARGE EGGS

1½ CUPS / 300 G SUGAR

1⅔ CUPS / 200 G ALL-PURPOSE FLOUR

1 TEASPOON FLEUR DE SEL

1 TEASPOON VANILLA EXTRACT

A HANDFUL OF RED BERRIES OR CURRANTS (OPTIONAL)

CONFECTIONERS' SUGAR, FOR SERVING

1. Preheat the oven to 325°F / 160°C. Grease a 9-inch / 23 cm cake pan with butter and line the bottom with a round of parchment paper.

2. Pour an inch or two of water into a medium saucepan and bring to a simmer. Combine the butter and chocolate in a heatproof bowl and set on top of the pan of simmering water. Stir until the butter and chocolate are melted. Remove from the heat and let cool for 10 minutes.

3. In a medium bowl, whisk together the eggs and sugar until light and fluffy. In another bowl, sift the flour and add the fleur de sel.

4. Stir the melted chocolate mixture into the egg mixture. Add the vanilla. Fold in the flour until just combined. Pour the batter into the prepared cake pan and bake for about 30 minutes.

5. Let cool in the pan for at least 1 hour before unmolding. Serve topped with berries, if desired, and a sprinkling of confectioners' sugar.

WALNUT CAKE

SERVES 8

This is without a doubt the recipe in this book that I've cooked most often this past year. We baked it for all the workshops, almost every day for the restaurant, and, in between, for ourselves. When you look over the list of recipes in the book you might not think this was the showstopper; so many others jump out first, seemingly richer, more delicious. But there is more to this cake than meets the eye. First of all, it's delicious but not too sweet, which is nice in and of itself, but it also means that Oddur has the excuse to serve a small glass of sweet wine, maybe an old Pineau from the Charentes, which goes incredibly well with the deep nutty flavor of the cake. Those who like whipped cream won't be disappointed because I serve it with a generous dollop on the side. This cake may not generate too much excitement beforehand, but after you've had it you'll fall in love. And that is the best sort of food love, not just a quick crush, but love that lasts.

5½ TABLESPOONS / 80 G UNSALTED BUTTER, PLUS MORE FOR THE PAN

1 CUP / 150 G WALNUTS, PLUS 5 WALNUT HALVES FOR DECORATING THE CAKE

⅔ CUP / 130 G GRANULATED SUGAR

3 LARGE EGGS

3 TABLESPOONS DARK RUM

1 TABLESPOON HONEY, PLUS MORE FOR DRIZZLING

½ TEASPOON VANILLA EXTRACT

PINCH OF FINE SEA SALT

⅓ CUP / 40 G ALL-PURPOSE FLOUR, SIFTED

¼ CUP / 30 G CORNSTARCH

1 TEASPOON BAKING POWDER

CONFECTIONERS' SUGAR

WHIPPED CREAM, FOR SERVING

1. Preheat the oven to 350°F / 180°C. Grease a 7-inch / 18 cm Bundt pan with butter.

2. Finely chop the walnuts or pulse them in a food processor until you have coarse crumbs. In a large bowl, combine the walnuts and granulated sugar and mix well. Mix in the butter, eggs, rum, honey, vanilla, and salt.

3. In another bowl, whisk together the flour, cornstarch, and baking powder. Fold the dry ingredients into the walnut mixture.

4. Pour the batter into the prepared pan. Bake until a knife inserted in the center comes out clean, about 40 minutes. Unmold and let cool for 10 minutes.

5. Sprinkle a dash of confectioners' sugar into a small sauté pan and add the 5 reserved walnut halves. Cook over medium-low heat for a few seconds, until the nuts are slightly golden. Arrange the walnuts on top of the warm cake and drizzle with a little honey before serving. Serve with whipped cream.

PLUM PAIN PERDU

SERVES 4

I get into French toast phases. I might not make any for months and then I suddenly make it three times in the same week. I really love the idea of taking bread that is slightly past its best and reviving it with simple ingredients, like eggs, milk, and butter. It's also practical when you live in the countryside and can't make it every morning to the bakery, which is in another village. Most often I make a classic version for breakfast, and sometimes I serve it with really good bacon and sausages. When I serve French toast as dessert, it is in plum season—and I call it *pain perdu*. Reviving "lost bread" with milk and eggs is very nice, but reviving it with a gorgeous, deep-red, syrupy plum compote not only gives it new life but also plunges it straight into a beautiful fairy tale.

FOR THE PLUM COMPOTE

10 PLUMS, HALVED AND PITTED

2 TABLESPOONS CONFECTIONERS' SUGAR

1 TABLESPOON / 15 G UNSALTED BUTTER

1 CINNAMON STICK

1 STAR ANISE

2 TABLESPOONS ORANGE FLOWER WATER

FOR THE PAIN PERDU

2 LARGE EGGS

2 TABLESPOONS GRANULATED SUGAR

1 CUP / 240 ML CRÈME FRAÎCHE

⅓ CUP / 80 ML WHOLE MILK

1 VANILLA BEAN, SPLIT LENGTHWISE, SEEDS SCRAPED AND RESERVED

8 SLICES BRIOCHE BREAD, 1 INCH / 2.5 CM THICK

4 TABLESPOONS / 60 G SALTED BUTTER

2 TABLESPOONS CONFECTIONERS' SUGAR (OPTIONAL)

1. **MAKE THE PLUM COMPOTE.** In a medium saucepan, combine the plums, confectioners' sugar, unsalted butter, cinnamon, and star anise and simmer over medium heat until the plums have softened, 5 to 10 minutes. Remove from the heat. The compote can be served warm or at room temperature. When ready to serve, discard the cinnamon and star anise and stir in the orange flower water.

2. **MEANWHILE, START THE PAIN PERDU.** In a large bowl, whisk together the eggs and granulated sugar. Whisk in the crème fraîche and milk. Add the vanilla seeds and continue to whisk until the batter is light and fluffy.

3. Soak the brioche slices in the batter for a few seconds on each side.

4. In a large sauté pan, melt half of the salted butter over medium heat. When the butter starts to sizzle, cook half of the bread until browned, about 1 minute on each side. Repeat with the remaining butter and brioche slices.

5. Serve immediately, topping each piece of pain perdu with a few spoons of the plum compote and a sprinkling of confectioners' sugar, if desired.

CHEESE

NO 1 RUE DE LOUDENNE had no big menu, no impressive cheese cart. We had an ever-changing *carte du jour* that offered the freshest we could find. Our guests had a choice of two starters, two mains, and two desserts. Officially there was no cheese. Like the oysters, the sausages, the radishes, and Champagne, the cheese was a little something extra. We wanted every night to be different, and, truthfully, sometimes we offered no cheese at all. Some nights we served guests a slice of excellent Camembert before dessert; sometimes there was a selection. Other times the only cheese of the evening came at the beginning: goat cheese canapés. Often we offered port or even opened a new bottle of wine just for the cheese.

One time, a whole evening was saved by a simple cheese from the Basque country. A demanding but otherwise very charming lady simply wasn't in the mood for dessert. "I hate sweets," she said. "I'd like a cheese platter instead." How do you explain to a woman who "hates sweets" that there was no cheese left in the house and she'd just have to stuff herself with chocolate cake or forever hold her peace? The answer is you don't. In the very back of our second fridge, the one where we store all the Champagne and meats, Oddur found a mature Ossau-iraty that had been hiding there for I do not know how long. It was only a couple of slices' worth, rather pungent, but possibly delicious. Oddur made an executive decision, slathered it in a traditional cherry jam we found in one of our cupboards, and presented it, with fanfare, on a huge serving dish. Had the lady asked for more, the answer would have been no; luckily that portion was enough for her. The lady who hated sweets finished it all, including the sweet cherry jam.

BABA AU RHUM

∾ SERVE 6 TO 8 ∾

As a young girl I had this deep fascination with *baba au rhum*. I could try to say that it was the beguiling shape, or the whipped cream that comes with the cake, but in honesty it was the rum that held all the intrigue. I saw people having *baba au rhum* in bistros and restaurants, but I was never allowed to have any, which only heightened my curiosity. Once my grandmother told my parents to let me try a little slice. "She won't like it anyway," she said. They hesitantly followed her advice. But my grandmother was wrong: I loved it. Which is funny, because I don't like rum as a drink—but in desserts it's pure heaven, especially when paired with cream.

FOR THE BABA

2 TABLESPOONS / 30 G UNSALTED
BUTTER, PLUS MORE FOR THE PAN

1⅔ CUPS / 200 G ALL-PURPOSE
FLOUR, PLUS MORE FOR THE PAN

3 TABLESPOONS WHOLE MILK

1 VANILLA BEAN, SPLIT LENGTHWISE,
SEEDS SCRAPED AND RESERVED

1 TABLESPOON / 10 G BAKING
POWDER

PINCH OF FINE SEA SALT

2 LARGE EGG YOLKS

½ CUP / 100 G GRANULATED SUGAR

2 LARGE EGG WHITES

FOR THE RUM SYRUP

½ CUP / 100 G GRANULATED SUGAR

¾ CUP / 180 ML DARK RUM

1 CUP / 240 ML HEAVY CREAM

2 TABLESPOONS CONFECTIONERS'
SUGAR

1. Preheat the oven to 350°F / 180°C. Grease a 3-cup / 800 ml Bundt pan with butter and sprinkle with flour. Shake out the excess over a sink.

2. **MAKE THE BABA.** In a saucepan, combine the milk, butter, and vanilla bean and seeds over medium heat until hot but not boiling.

3. Meanwhile, sift together the flour, baking powder, and salt.

4. In a large bowl, whisk together the egg yolks and granulated sugar until smooth. Whisk in the hot milk mixture and then the flour mixture.

5. Using an electric mixer, whip the egg whites until they hold stiff peaks. Gently fold them into the batter.

6. Pour the batter into the prepared pan and bake until golden brown and a knife inserted in the baba comes out clean, about 30 minutes. Let cool for 10 minutes and then unmold onto a rimmed serving platter.

7. **PREPARE THE RUM SYRUP.** In a small saucepan, bring the granulated sugar and ½ cup / 120 ml water to a boil. Add the rum, reduce the heat, and simmer just until the sugar dissolves.

8. Whip the cream and confectioners' sugar until the cream holds stiff peaks.

9. Slowly pour the rum syrup all over the cake and wait until it is fully absorbed. Serve with the whipped cream and a drizzle of any pooled rum syrup, if desired.

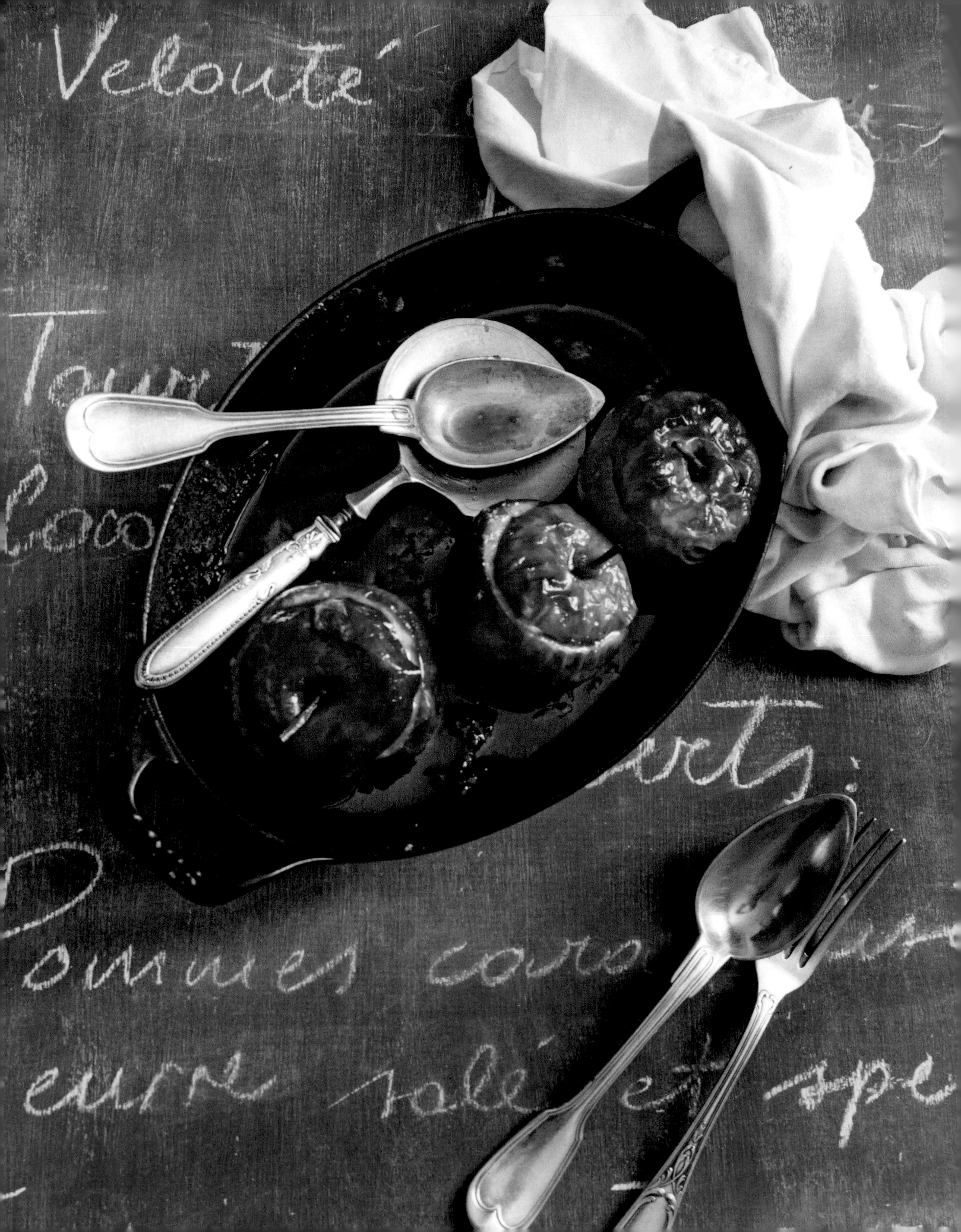
Velouté

BAKED APPLES WITH SPÉCULOOS

*S*péculoos are simple, tasty, spiced cookies you can find almost everywhere in various versions and different levels of quality. I've always liked to play around with them, include them in tarts and desserts. They go very well with pears, apples, and plums; in summer I like to make a plum tart with a *spéculoos*-crusted base. In the months leading up to Christmas, we have so many apples around the house that I like to put them to use, often in tarts but also on their own, which I find is a chic way to serve them. This is a humble, uncomplicated dessert, perfect for the days before Christmas, when you have no time to make an elaborate recipe but are aching for a little sweet something to round off a meal.

8 APPLES

6½ TABLESPOONS / 90 G UNSALTED
BUTTER

8 SPÉCULOOS COOKIES

¼ CUP / 50 G SUGAR

1. Preheat the oven to 400°F / 200°C.

2. Slice off the top part of the apples, making a little "hat," and core the apples, leaving a little of the bottom intact. Put the apples in a baking dish and stick about 1 teaspoon of butter into the center of each. Crumble a *spéculoos* cookie into each one and divide the remaining butter among the apples, dabbing it on top of the cookie. Sprinkle the sugar over the apples and top the apples with their "hats."

3. Transfer the dish to the oven and bake until the apples are golden and tender, about 25 minutes. Serve immediately.

STRAWBERRY TART

S trawberries, like cherries, peaches, and plums, only ever enter my kitchen in summer. By now I have so many different recipes for them, each more delicious than the next, that I often forget about this grand original, the strawberry tart. I have farmer friends who live nearby and they grow the finest strawberries I've ever had, but they're fragile and don't travel well. Nor do they last very long, so we try to eat them all in one day. In season we eat the first batches straight out of the box, and then I soon turn to my strawberry repertoire. Every single time I make this tart I am surprised at how good it is, which is undoubtedly why it became a classic in the first place. I do have a little twist: I use lime instead of lemon for the pastry cream, which makes the tart super refreshing and tangy.

ALL-PURPOSE FLOUR

SWEET TART DOUGH (FROM
PLANTIA'S TARTE TATIN, PAGE 22)

⅔ CUP / 130 G SUGAR

3 LARGE EGG YOLKS

1 LARGE EGG

¼ CUP / 30 G CORNSTARCH, SIFTED

1 CUP / 240 ML WHOLE MILK

1 TEASPOON VANILLA EXTRACT

1 TABLESPOON GRATED LIME ZEST

3 TABLESPOONS FRESH LIME JUICE

3 TABLESPOONS RED CURRANT
JELLY

1 POUND / 450 G STRAWBERRIES

MINT LEAVES, FOR SERVING
(OPTIONAL)

1. On a lightly floured work surface, roll out the dough to a 12-inch / 30 cm round that's ¼ inch / 6 mm thick. Fit into the base and up the sides of a 10-inch / 25 cm tart pan. Trim off any excess dough. Prick the base all over with a fork. Cover with plastic wrap and freeze for 30 minutes to prevent shrinkage during baking.

2. Preheat the oven to 400°F / 200°C.

3. Line the tart shell with parchment paper and fill with pie weights or dried beans. Bake until the sides start to turn golden brown, about 15 minutes. Remove from the oven and remove the pie weights. Return the tart shell to the oven and continue to bake until the base is golden, about 5 minutes. Set aside to cool.

4. In a large bowl, whisk together the sugar, egg yolks, and whole egg. Whisk in the cornstarch.

5. In a medium saucepan, bring the milk to a low simmer over medium heat. Slowly pour the milk into the egg mixture, whisking constantly. Whisk in the vanilla and lime zest.

6. Return the mixture to the saucepan, whisk in the lime juice, and cook over medium heat, whisking constantly, until the mixture has thickened to a custard and boils for 30 seconds to 1 minute. Pour the cream into a bowl and cover with plastic wrap pressed directly on the surface of the cream so it does not form a skin. Let cool and then refrigerate until cold, at least 3 hours or overnight.

7. In a small saucepan, heat the red currant jelly with 1 tablespoon water over medium-low heat, stirring occasionally, until melted and smooth, a minute or two. Remove from the heat and set aside to cool.

8. Spoon the lime custard into the tart shell and smooth with a spatula. Decorate with the strawberries. With a pastry brush, brush the tart shell and the strawberries with the red currant glaze. Serve immediately, topped with mint leaves, if desired, or refrigerate for up to 4 hours before serving.

RASPBERRY SOUFFLÉ

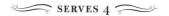

SERVES 4

Every French cookbook needs a soufflé or two, preferably a sweet one and a savory one. I think at this stage in my life I've made about every possible type of soufflé that you can make, or at least that I want to make, so picking two for this book was no easy task. Quite early on I decided on a White Asparagus Soufflé (page 112)—so special, seasonal, and delicious. But the sweet one was trickier. Chocolate soufflés are wonderful, but I was already set on Chocolate Ice Cream (page 315) and they felt too similar. A classic Grand Marnier soufflé is tasty, too, and always feels so appropriate. I almost picked that one. But then I started imagining a menu, a lunch that I'd be invited to, with a dream lineup of dishes. The starter would be Endive, Roquefort, and Walnut Salad (page 234), the main course Monkfish Stew with Saffron (page 169), and for dessert a soufflé, a blackberry soufflé with vanilla ice cream. No, wait, a beautiful, golden pink raspberry soufflé—even better.

2 TABLESPOONS / 30 G UNSALTED
BUTTER, PLUS MORE FOR THE
RAMEKINS

2 TABLESPOONS ALL-PURPOSE
FLOUR, PLUS MORE FOR THE
RAMEKINS

2 TABLESPOONS CORNSTARCH

¾ CUP PLUS 1 TABLESPOON / 195 ML
WHOLE MILK

½ VANILLA BEAN, SPLIT
LENGTHWISE, SEEDS SCRAPED
AND RESERVED

3 LARGE EGG YOLKS

5 OUNCES / 150 G FRESH
RASPBERRIES, CRUSHED WITH A
FORK, PLUS WHOLE RASPBERRIES,
FOR SERVING

3 LARGE EGG WHITES

PINCH OF FINE SEA SALT

3 TABLESPOONS SUGAR

1. Preheat the oven to 400°F / 200°C. Butter 4 (7-ounce / 210 ml) ramekins and sprinkle with flour. Tap the ramekins over a sink to remove excess flour. Put the ramekins in the freezer until needed.

2. In a large saucepan, melt the 2 tablespoons butter over medium-low heat. Whisk in the flour and cornstarch. Immediately pour in the milk, add the vanilla bean seeds, and continue to whisk until the mixture thickens to a custard, coating the back of a spoon, 5 to 8 minutes.

3. Remove the pan from the heat and whisk in the egg yolks and then the raspberries.

4. Using an electric mixer, whip the egg whites until frothy, then add the salt. Continue to whip on high speed, gradually adding the sugar, until the whites hold stiff peaks. Fold the egg whites into the raspberry mixture.

5. Take the ramekins out of the freezer and fill them to ½ inch / 1.3 cm from the top with the raspberry mixture. Put on a baking sheet and bake until risen and golden brown on top, about 15 minutes. Serve immediately, topping each with a raspberry.

CHERRY STEW

SERVES 6

A thing I both love and hate about cherries is how seldom I can get them. That sounds weird, I know. If you like something, shouldn't you want it all the time? I see that point, of course, but it's the rarity that makes them special and even more appreciated. The first cherries usually come around my husband's birthday in early May, and we always buy some even if that means paying through the nose. These we eat out of hand, just how they came off the tree. Slowly the price goes down, and we start buying more and more, mountains' worth actually, meaning some are left for me to cook, such as in this easy cherry dessert, which is lovely spooned over Almond Ice Cream (page 306). For a few weeks our lives are saturated in cherries—they are all around, on tables, in bowls, in most meals we have—and then they're gone. That's when I move on to peaches, then plums. When cherries reappear in stores in December, imported because it's Christmas, I never touch them, not just because the price isn't right. It's more that the time isn't right. Cherries in December are like tomatoes in February: out of place.

3 TABLESPOONS / 45 G UNSALTED BUTTER

4 POUNDS / 1.8 KG CHERRIES, STEMMED

¼ CUP / 50 G SUGAR

¼ CUP / 60 ML ORANGE FLOWER WATER

A FEW FRESH MINT LEAVES, CHOPPED

1. In a large, deep sauté pan or shallow pot, melt the butter over medium heat. When the butter starts to foam, add the cherries. Sprinkle the sugar over the top and cook for 3 minutes.

2. Pour in the orange flower water and simmer to reduce until the sauce is thick like a syrup, about 1 minute.

3. Serve the warm cherries in individual dessert coupes, pouring the sauce all over. Scatter the mint leaves on top.

ORANGE BLOSSOM CAKE

SERVES 6

Those who know me well, and perhaps even those who don't, know about my fondness for orange flower water. I would put it in practically everything if I could: in breads and cakes, salads and sauces. I even spray some on my bed linens, put it behind the children's ears after a bath, and generally live by it. It's the perfume of my life. A cake doesn't really need much more than orange flower water to be a success, but this one has another helper: crème fraîche, which replaces the usual butter. It's the cake I'd make on a Monday evening for a light dessert, just because it's Monday.

UNSALTED BUTTER

FOR THE CAKE

3 LARGE EGGS

1 CUP / 200 G GRANULATED SUGAR

5 TABLESPOONS / 75 ML ORANGE
FLOWER WATER

¾ CUP / 180 ML CRÈME FRAÎCHE

2 CUPS / 250 G ALL-PURPOSE
FLOUR, SIFTED

1 TEASPOON BAKING POWDER

FOR THE FROSTING

8 TABLESPOONS / 120 G UNSALTED
BUTTER, AT ROOM TEMPERATURE

2 CUPS / 200 G CONFECTIONERS'
SUGAR

⅔ CUP / 160 ML HEAVY CREAM

1 TABLESPOON ORANGE FLOWER
WATER

¼ TEASPOON VANILLA EXTRACT

ORANGE BLOSSOMS OR OTHER
EDIBLE FLOWERS (OPTIONAL)

1. Preheat the oven to 350°F / 180°C. Butter an 8-inch / 20 cm cake pan.

2. **MAKE THE CAKE.** Using an electric mixer, whip the eggs and granulated sugar until light in color and fluffy, about 5 minutes.

3. Whisk in the orange flower water and then mix in the crème fraîche. Add the flour and baking powder and whisk until the batter is light and smooth.

4. Pour the batter into the prepared pan. Bake until the cake has risen, is golden brown, and a knife inserted in the center comes out clean, about 35 minutes. Cool in the pan on a wire rack for 5 minutes, then unmold to cool completely.

5. **MAKE THE FROSTING.** Using an electric mixer, beat together the butter and confectioners' sugar until light and fluffy, about 3 minutes. Add the heavy cream, orange flower water, and vanilla and beat until the frosting is silky smooth.

6. Spread the frosting on top of the cooled cake and decorate with orange blossoms, if desired.

BAKED PEARS WITH CHOCOLATE

SERVES 8

I n the early days of our marriage I spent a few Christmases in Iceland and got to know the local traditions. On Christmas Day Icelandic people like to have very salty lamb, which they call "hanging meat," and serve it with a creamy potato stew. On the side they always have flatbread that families bake and decorate as part of the holiday preparations. Dessert is often a rich meringue cake, stuffed with cream and all sorts of sweets, like chocolate-covered raisins and pralines. But there are also other classic desserts, like the one my mother-in-law makes with canned pears, melted After Eight mint chocolates, and whipped cream. Her version doesn't really need to be improved on, but I do like to make it with fresh pears, now that most of us can get them at Christmastime.

8 FIRM-RIPE MEDIUM PEARS

3 TABLESPOONS / 45 G UNSALTED BUTTER, MELTED

2 TABLESPOONS HONEY

5 OUNCES / 150 G DARK CHOCOLATE (AT LEAST 70% CACAO), COARSELY CHOPPED

A HANDFUL OF FRESH MINT LEAVES

1. Preheat the oven to 350°F / 180°C.

2. Peel the pears, if desired (pears are better unpeeled), and halve them, scooping out the seeds but leaving the stems intact. Arrange the pears cut side up in a baking dish just large enough to hold them. Drizzle melted butter and honey on each halved pear.

3. Bake the pears until tender and golden, about 25 minutes.

4. Pour a couple of inches of water in a saucepan and bring to a simmer over medium-high heat. Put the chocolate in a heatproof bowl and set over the saucepan of simmering water to melt. Remove from the heat and stir until smooth and glossy.

5. Just before serving, drizzle the chocolate sauce over the pears and scatter the mint leaves on top. Serve warm.

ROASTED PEACHES WITH PISTACHIO CREAM

 SERVES 4

I have purposely stayed away from the word *ultimate* while writing this book, but here it comes: This is the ultimate summer dessert. After a day at the beach, when the family is happy and sun-kissed, when we are joined by dear friends for a casual feast of barbecue and wine, there is no other dessert that comes close to this one. It's certainly one of the easiest recipes in the book, which is exactly what you're looking for when you're cooking for an army of people after a long day of swimming. I recruit the kids to halve and pit the peaches. Those who have grilled the meat usually get a break from the barbecue, and we send in a different team to roast the peaches in the oven, often one of the older kids. Then I whip the cream and apply the final touch with the pistachios. It's teamwork, family style.

1 VANILLA BEAN, SPLIT LENGTHWISE, SEEDS SCRAPED AND RESERVED

4 LARGE PEACHES, HALVED AND PITTED

8 TEASPOONS UNSALTED BUTTER

3 TABLESPOONS HONEY

½ CUP / 120 ML HEAVY CREAM

2 TABLESPOONS CONFECTIONERS' SUGAR

A LARGE HANDFUL OF PISTACHIOS, COARSELY CHOPPED

1. Preheat the oven to 425°F / 210°C.

2. Rub the vanilla seeds onto the cut sides of the peach halves. Put the peaches, cut side up, in an ovenproof skillet and add a teaspoon of butter to the center of each one. Drizzle with the honey and transfer to the oven. Bake until tender, 8 to 10 minutes.

3. Meanwhile, whip the cream until it holds soft peaks and then incorporate the confectioners' sugar and pistachios, reserving a few nuts for garnish. Serve the warm peaches sprinkled with the reserved nuts and with the pistachio whipped cream on the side.

CHERRY AND ALMOND CAKE

SERVES 6 TO 8

Usually I don't construct menus that are too heavily focused on one or two ingredients, but this is the cake I make frequently at the height of cherry season when we've often already had something with cherries during the day. Cherries pair wonderfully with almonds, and though you could easily serve this cake with a good vanilla ice cream, I think almond ice cream makes it more special. If I may make a suggestion, I'd propose serving this cake at a cherry-themed, midsummer's night dinner, after the Roast Duck with Cherries (page 142). In the duck dish the cherries are perfumed by the duck and get mixed up in the sauce and potatoes. In the cake they show a completely different side and merge perfectly with the almond flavors.

11 TABLESPOONS / 160 G UNSALTED BUTTER, MELTED, PLUS MORE FOR THE PAN

1½ CUPS / 180 GRAMS ALL-PURPOSE FLOUR, PLUS MORE FOR THE PAN

1 CUP / 120 G ALMOND FLOUR

⅔ CUP / 130 G GRANULATED SUGAR

3 LARGE EGGS

1 TEASPOON ALMOND EXTRACT

1 TEASPOON BAKING POWDER

PINCH OF FINE SEA SALT

10 OUNCES / 300 G CHERRIES, STEMMED AND PITTED

⅓ CUP / 50 G SLIVERED ALMONDS

2 TABLESPOONS LIGHT BROWN SUGAR

ALMOND ICE CREAM (PAGE 306; OPTIONAL), FOR SERVING

1. Preheat the oven to 350°F / 180°C. Butter a 9-inch / 23 cm springform pan and dust with all-purpose flour. Tap out the excess flour.

2. In a medium bowl, mix together the melted butter, almond flour, and granulated sugar to make a smooth paste. Incorporate the eggs and almond extract.

3. In another bowl, sift together the all-purpose flour, baking powder, and salt. Fold the dry ingredients into the almond batter. Gently add the cherries, distributing them evenly into the batter with your spatula.

4. Pour the batter into the prepared pan and bake for 30 minutes.

5. Remove the cake from the oven and scatter the almonds and brown sugar on top. Return to the oven and continue to bake until the top is golden and a knife inserted into the center comes out clean, about 10 minutes. Let cool in the pan on a wire rack for 10 minutes before unmolding and cooling completely. Serve with almond ice cream, if desired.

ALMOND ICE CREAM

~ MAKES 1 QUART / 1 LITER ~

1 CUP / 150 G ALMONDS

¾ CUP / 150 G SUGAR

2 CUPS / 480 ML HEAVY CREAM

1 CUP / 240 ML WHOLE MILK

½ TEASPOON VANILLA EXTRACT

½ TEASPOON ALMOND EXTRACT

¼ TEASPOON FINE SEA SALT

5 LARGE EGG YOLKS

1. Preheat the oven to 350°F / 180°F. Line a baking sheet with parchment paper.

2. Spread the almonds on the baking sheet and bake until golden brown, 10 to 12 minutes. Set aside to cool.

3. In a food processor, combine the almonds and sugar and pulse until finely ground, about 1 minute.

4. In a large saucepan, combine the almond mixture, cream, milk, vanilla and almond extracts, and salt. Stir well and bring to a low boil over medium heat. Remove from the heat and let cool for 1 minute.

5. In a medium bowl, whisk the egg yolks. Slowly whisk in some of the cream mixture to warm the yolks. Whisk the yolk mixture back into the saucepan and return to low heat. Continue to cook, whisking, until the mixture has thickened to a custard, coating the back of a spoon, 1 to 2 minutes. Do not boil. Transfer to a bowl and let cool completely. Cover with plastic wrap and refrigerate for at least 2 hours or, preferably, overnight.

6. Freeze the almond cream in an ice cream machine according to the manufacturer's instructions. Scoop the ice cream into a container, cover, and freeze for at least 3 hours before serving.

PRUNE PARCELS

SERVES 6

Irealize that I keep talking about my grandmother and my aunt Taty. My summers were largely spent in their kitchens, and they played a big part in my food upbringing. I was the little, skinny, foreign-looking kid in the corner, carefully observing their every move, breathing in the wonderful aromas and perfumes, anticipating food different from what I ate in Hong Kong. The South of France, where my aunt lives, is famous for a special variety of grape called Chasselas, and not far from there is Agen, the prune capital of France. When I was selecting recipes for the book, I planned on having a recipe for prunes in Armagnac, one of the most iconic desserts from the region. Instead I opted for this recipe, still with prunes, but no Armagnac, just because I think you will enjoy it more. The hot prune compote, the crispy phyllo pastry, the melting vanilla ice cream—I'm sure I made the right choice!

2 CUPS / 300 G PRUNES, PITTED

½ CUP / 120 ML ORANGE FLOWER WATER

2 TABLESPOONS HONEY

6 SHEETS FROZEN PHYLLO (FILO) PASTRY, THAWED

2 TABLESPOONS / 30 G UNSALTED BUTTER, MELTED

VANILLA ICE CREAM, FOR SERVING

1. Preheat the oven to 350°F / 180°C. Line a baking sheet with parchment paper.

2. In a medium saucepan, combine the prunes, ½ cup / 120 ml water, the orange flower water, and honey and bring to a simmer over medium heat. Reduce the heat, cover, and cook until the prunes are very soft and tender, about 10 minutes. Mash the prunes with a fork and set aside to cool.

3. Unwrap one sheet of phyllo pastry and cut off part of one side to make a square. Scoop a tablespoon of prunes in the center. Fold the phyllo up around the prunes to make a parcel and then tie it closed with kitchen twine. Transfer to the baking sheet and brush with a little of the melted butter. Repeat with the remaining phyllo, prunes, and butter.

4. Bake until the parcels are golden brown, about 8 minutes. Serve immediately with a scoop of vanilla ice cream.

WALNUT TART

~ SERVES 6 TO 8 ~

Walnuts are a product of autumn, like mushrooms and pumpkins, and I like to put them into that context in a fall menu. That's a thing I do often: think of how a dish goes with the other dishes. Something may be great on its own; other things need an opening, and that's how I think of this tart. I'd start with Pumpkin Quiche with Bacon (page 104) and a glass of white Bordeaux, a crispy, well-chilled Sauvignon Blanc that goes incredibly well with the soup. Then I'd make Wild Mushrooms with an Egg Yolk (page 113) and open a big, Médoc-style red, not necessarily too old but ready to drink. Then I'd serve this tart, so delicious with the caramelized walnuts, and maybe, just maybe, pair it with Sauternes wine.

FOR THE DOUGH

1½ CUPS / 180 G ALL-PURPOSE
FLOUR, PLUS MORE FOR ROLLING

½ TEASPOON SUGAR

½ TEASPOON FINE SEA SALT

8 TABLESPOONS / 120 G UNSALTED
BUTTER, CUT INTO SMALL CUBES

2 TABLESPOONS ICE WATER

FOR THE FILLING

1⅔ CUPS / 250 G WALNUT HALVES

½ CUP / 120 ML HONEY

2 TABLESPOONS / 30 G UNSALTED
BUTTER

¼ CUP / 50 G SUGAR

1 TEASPOON VANILLA EXTRACT

2 LARGE EGGS, LIGHTLY BEATEN

1. **MAKE THE DOUGH.** In a food processor, combine the flour, sugar, salt, butter, and ice water. Pulse for 10 to 20 seconds, or until you get a smooth dough. Shape into a ball, wrap in plastic wrap, and refrigerate for at least 1 hour or overnight.

2. On a lightly floured work surface, roll out the dough to a 12-inch / 30 cm round ¼ inch / 5 mm thick. Fit into the base and up the sides of a 10-inch / 25 cm tart pan. Trim off any excess dough. Prick the base all over with a fork. Cover with plastic wrap and freeze for 30 minutes to prevent shrinkage during baking.

3. **MAKE THE FILLING.** Preheat the oven to 350°F / 180°C. Line a baking sheet with parchment paper.

4. Put the walnuts on the baking sheet and roast in the oven until golden, about 8 minutes. Set aside to cool.

5. In a large saucepan, warm the honey and butter over medium-low heat until melted. Remove from the heat and let cool for 5 minutes. Mix in the walnuts, sugar, and vanilla. Mix in the eggs.

6. Pour the filling into the tart shell and bake until golden brown, about 40 minutes. Let cool completely on a wire rack before serving.

CRÊPES SUZETTE

I have friends whose first order of business, when they get off the plane in Paris, is to rush to their favorite (or the nearest) crêpe vendor and order themselves delicious crêpes Suzette. I don't blame them; I used to do the same. When I was a teenager, having crêpes Suzette in a café in Paris by myself meant being a little bit grown-up. Later, as a student living in the city, I would often go to a café after school, typically one in the Marais district, and order myself the best crêpes Suzette in town, drenched in orange liqueur sauce. I'd sit there for longer than I needed (eating pancakes beats studying), and I always left feeling supremely satisfied.

Now that I live in the countryside, cafés that make crêpes Suzette are few and far between. So I make them myself every so often when the mood strikes me—for breakfast, after a meal, or even as a meal. It's the perfect thing to have when I want to feel like a young girl in Paris or when I have friends who are fresh off the plane.

FOR THE CRÊPES

2 TABLESPOONS / 30 G UNSALTED BUTTER, PLUS MORE FOR THE PAN

SCANT 1 CUP / 110 G ALL-PURPOSE FLOUR, SIFTED

1 TABLESPOON SUGAR

½ TEASPOON FINE SEA SALT

1 LARGE EGG

1 CUP / 240 ML WHOLE MILK

½ TEASPOON VANILLA EXTRACT

1 TABLESPOON ORANGE LIQUEUR

GRATED ZEST OF 1 ORANGE

GRATED ZEST OF 1 LEMON

1. **START THE CRÊPE BATTER.** In an 8-inch / 20 cm skillet, melt the 2 tablespoons butter over medium heat. Remove from the heat and set aside to cool.

2. In a large bowl, mix together the flour, sugar, and salt. Whisk in the egg, milk, and vanilla to make a smooth batter. Whisk in the melted butter, orange liqueur, orange zest, and lemon zest. Cover with plastic wrap and refrigerate for at least 1 hour or overnight.

3. Grease the small skillet and return it to medium-high heat. When the pan is very hot, spoon 1½ tablespoons of the batter into the pan, swirling the pan to cover the surface evenly. Cook for a minute or so, until the edges start browning. Lift the edges slightly with a butter knife, then flip the pancake and brown the other side, about 30 seconds.

4. Transfer to a plate and continue cooking the remaining batter in the same fashion, stacking the crêpes on top of each other. You should get 20 to 25 crêpes. When finished, cover the stack with an inverted plate, wrap in a clean kitchen towel, and cover with plastic wrap or a plastic bag to keep the pancakes moist and soft. You can keep the crêpes this way for up to 6 hours before serving.

FOR THE BUTTER SAUCE

GRATED ZEST AND JUICE
OF 2 ORANGES

1 TABLESPOON FRESH LEMON JUICE

½ CUP / 100 G SUGAR

8 TABLESPOONS / 120 G
COLD UNSALTED BUTTER,
CUT INTO PIECES

5 TABLESPOONS ORANGE LIQUEUR

5. **MAKE THE BUTTER SAUCE.** In a saucepan, combine the orange juice, lemon juice, and sugar and bring to a simmer over medium heat. Simmer until the mixture thickens to a syrup, about 8 minutes. Gradually whisk in the butter and orange liqueur until incorporated. Do not boil.

6. To serve, fold each crêpe in half and in half again to form a triangle. Serve immediately, topped with the warm sauce and the orange zest.

CHOCOLATE ICE CREAM

～ SERVES 6 ～

A few years ago we were invited for lunch at a château in nearby St Estèphe. Rather than bringing us to the dining room, the host, Basil Tesseron, showed us to the kitchen at Château Lafon-Rochet, his family's estate. There we were joined by Basil's wife, Bérangère, whose family also owns a château (yes, it's like that in Médoc) and another young couple whose family has one in Sauternes. It was a wonderfully casual affair: The lunch was prepared by the housekeeper, lovely veal and vegetables, and served with a few bottles of his and hers wines. For dessert, Basil, beaming with pride, served us the darkest, richest chocolate ice cream you could ever imagine. He had made it himself and—perhaps to honor his cousin, the Sauternes maker, or simply because he likes it—he paired the ice cream with a well-chilled, deliciously sweet glass of Sauternes. The pairing was perfect and reaffirmed my belief that some of the very best meals are had in friends' kitchens. I always meant to get Basil's recipe but somehow never got around to it, so I made my own version, which I think is equally as good. I don't always pair this ice cream with Sauternes—unless I have guests; then I like to surprise them, especially if we're eating in the kitchen.

8 OUNCES / 230 G UNSWEETENED CHOCOLATE

½ CUP / 70 G UNSWEETENED COCOA POWDER

8 TABLESPOONS / 120 G UNSALTED BUTTER, CUT INTO SMALL CUBES

1 TEASPOON VANILLA EXTRACT

PINCH OF FINE SEA SALT

¾ CUP / 150 G SUGAR

4 LARGE EGG YOLKS

2 CUPS / 500 ML HEAVY CREAM

1. In a heatproof bowl, break the chocolate into pieces and combine with the cocoa powder and butter. Pour a couple of inches of water into a saucepan and bring to a simmer over medium-high heat. Set the bowl over the gently simmering water and melt the chocolate. Remove from the heat and stir until smooth. Stir in the vanilla and salt.

2. In a saucepan, combine the sugar with ⅔ cup / 160 ml water. Heat over medium-low heat until the sugar dissolves and the syrup is clear. Remove from the heat and let cool for a minute.

3. Using an electric mixer, beat the egg yolks in a large bowl. Slowly pour the hot sugar syrup into the yolks while whipping constantly. Continue to whip until the mixture is thick and glossy and has cooled slightly. Pour in the cream and the melted chocolate mixture and continue to whisk until light and fluffy. Let cool completely before covering with plastic wrap and refrigerating until cold.

4. Freeze the chocolate mixture in an ice cream machine according to the manufacturer's instructions. Scoop the ice cream into a container, cover, and freeze for at least 3 hours before serving.

VANILLA MARSHMALLOWS

MAKES 10 MARSHMALLOWS

I love old-fashioned restaurants, with vintage silver, stiff white tablecloths, and, most critically, great food. It helps if the waiters are nice; they can have character and quirks, but ultimately they should make the diners feel welcome. When you keep revisiting the same restaurants, a bond forms: You get to know the staff, and they get to know you. Maybe they bring you a little coupe of Champagne when you are looking over the menu, or they'll make suggestions they know you'll like. One little trick that I always appreciate in restaurants is when they offer a little bonbon with the coffee, or even just with the bill, to sweeten the shock. Sometimes these treats are simple *cannelés*, sometimes little chocolates. But what really melts my heart is a shiny jar filled with homemade marshmallows. Maybe it's the kid in me, but that sort of little gesture usually wins me over for life.

½ CUP / 50 G CONFECTIONERS'
SUGAR

½ CUP / 50 G CORNSTARCH

VEGETABLE OIL

10 GELATIN SHEETS
OR 2 (¼-OUNCE) ENVELOPES
POWDERED GELATIN

2 LARGE EGG WHITES

2 CUPS / 400 G GRANULATED SUGAR

1 TABLESPOON VANILLA EXTRACT

1 VANILLA BEAN, SPLIT LENGTHWISE,
SEEDS SCRAPED AND RESERVED

1. In a bowl, sift together the confectioners' sugar and cornstarch. Lightly grease a 7 × 11-inch / 18 × 28 cm baking pan with vegetable oil, then dust generously with some of the confectioners' sugar mixture.

2. Soak the gelatin sheets in a bowl of ½ cup / 120 ml cold water or sprinkle the powdered gelatin over an equal amount of cold water to soften.

3. Using an electric mixer, whip the egg whites until they hold stiff peaks.

4. Meanwhile, in a medium saucepan, combine the granulated sugar and ¼ cup / 60 ml water. Using a candy thermometer, heat the mixture until it reaches 248°F / 120°C, the firm ball stage. Remove from the heat.

5. Drain the gelatin sheets, squeezing out excess water. Gently stir the gelatin (whichever kind you are using) into the hot sugar syrup until melted. Whipping on low speed, carefully drizzle the sugar/gelatin mixture into the egg whites, aiming for the side of the bowl. Add the vanilla extract and vanilla seeds. Whisk on high speed until the bowl is cool to the touch and the mixture is light and fluffy, 5 to 6 minutes.

6. Pour the marshmallow mixture into the prepared pan. Use a large spatula to spread it evenly. Dust some of the remaining confectioners' sugar mixture on top. Let set for 4 hours, uncovered, in a cool room.

7. Cut the marshmallow with a large knife or kitchen scissors into 1¼-inch / 3 cm cubes. Dust with the remaining confectioners' sugar mixture before serving. The marshmallows will keep in a covered container at room temperature for up to 5 days.

ALMOND TUILES

MAKES ABOUT 40 COOKIES

I have a pretend aunt who's not really nice—a great contrast to my real aunt who's the nicest woman in the world. This fantasy aunt, luckily, rarely visits; but when she announces her impending arrival (no, she doesn't wait for an invitation; she's that sort of aunt), she sends shivers through our household. Silver must be polished, floors waxed, children bathed. When she arrives, the house is at its best, every vase filled with the freshest flowers, every dog scrubbed and groomed to perfection. Still, that's not enough for her; she walks from room to room, giving us all a dismissive look as if to say, "I don't know why I bother coming to this pigsty." Then I invite her to our biggest dining room where I have laid out a tea service fit for a queen and pour her a perfectly brewed cup of the finest Assam tea. She sits there not knowing what to say, her facial expression indicating something between boredom and suffering. That's the time, in this otherwise delusional fantasy, that I bring out the almond tuiles. They must be freshly baked, they must be slightly crunchy but still with a hint of softness in the middle, though not too much. She takes a bite, then another. Now she has a second tuile. That's when she remembers why she keeps coming to our house.

4 LARGE EGG WHITES

1 CUP / 120 G ALL-PURPOSE FLOUR

½ CUP / 100 G SUPERFINE SUGAR

PINCH OF FINE SEA SALT

4 TABLESPOONS / 60 G UNSALTED
BUTTER, MELTED

1 TEASPOON ALMOND EXTRACT

½ TEASPOON VANILLA EXTRACT

⅓ CUP / 50 G SLIVERED ALMONDS

1. Preheat the oven to 400°F / 200°C. Line several baking sheets with parchment paper.

2. Using an electric mixer, whip the egg whites in a large bowl until they form medium peaks. In a separate bowl, whisk together the flour, sugar, and salt and gradually add to the whites. Add the melted butter and almond and vanilla extracts and whip until combined.

3. Using about 1 teaspoon of batter for each cookie, spread very thin rounds on the parchment-lined baking sheets. Sprinkle the slivered almonds on top of the tuiles. Bake in batches until the edges are golden brown, about 6 minutes.

4. The tuiles will set very quickly, so you'll have to be fast if you want to shape them (though they are equally delicious and admittedly less stressful when left flat). Use a thin spatula to lift each tuile and carefully place on a rolling pin or empty wine bottle to create a curved shape. Let cool completely before serving.

MERVEILLEUX

SERVES 6 TO 8

When it comes to cooking I think we all have our own little comfort zones where we feel most confident. For me that comfort zone is meringues. I've always liked them; to me there is no confection more beautiful or dreamy, and through the years I have bought more meringues in pastry shops and restaurants than I probably should have. When I started cooking for myself, I purposely sidestepped meringues for a while; if I were to fail, my world would be shattered. Gradually I gained some confidence and after numerous attempts mastered meringue making. And I don't talk about mastering things very often. The secret is that despite appearances they're quite simple to make, especially if you start with a good recipe. I make several versions of meringues, and this classic kind can often be found in pastry shops around France. Crispy on the outside, they are wonderful topped with cream and covered in chunky flakes of dark chocolate. As their name suggests, they're simply marvelous!

3 LARGE EGG WHITES

1 CUP / 100 G CONFECTIONERS'
SUGAR

½ CUP / 100 G SUPERFINE SUGAR

½ TEASPOON CORNSTARCH OR
CREAM OF TARTAR

1½ CUPS / 350 ML HEAVY CREAM

5 OUNCES / 150 G DARK CHOCOLATE

1. Preheat the oven to 275°F / 140°C. Line a baking sheet with parchment paper.

2. Using an electric mixer, whip the egg whites on high speed until frothy. Gradually (1 to 2 tablespoons at a time) add the confectioners' sugar, superfine sugar, and cornstarch and continue whipping until the whites are stiff and glossy. Transfer the mixture to a piping bag fitted with a small plain tip. Pipe 2½-inch / 6.5 cm round meringues, about the size of a round plum, onto the parchment-lined baking sheet.

3. Bake for 25 minutes. Reduce the oven temperature to 200°F / 95°C and continue to bake for 2 hours. Turn off the heat and open the oven door. Let the meringues cool completely in the oven, at least 1 hour or overnight.

4. To serve, whip the cream until it holds stiff peaks. Grate the chocolate into flakes (I use a vegetable peeler). Cover the meringues evenly with a thick layer of cream and sprinkle with the chocolate flakes. Serve immediately.

EPILOGUE

"This roof will last for a hundred years!" That's what Monsieur Ladra told us when he sold us the house. As work on the house turned out to be more than expected (far more, to be exact), I always took great comfort in his words. All new work was justified by *well, at least we won't have to change the roof.* We needed everything from new electricity to new shutters, but that's nothing compared with changing a roof.

One day the roof will have to be changed—in ninety-seven years, according to Monsieur Ladra, but probably closer to sixty or seventy. Either way, I won't be the one doing it or living through it, and for that I am thankful. I do think about it from time to time, though, imagining the start of work. A team of artisans will arrive at the gates of No 1 rue de Loudenne and walk past a magnificent magnolia tree, a few little white dogs, and so many olive trees that they will wonder who on earth decided to plant so many in such little space. Someone will show them to the roof to assess the slate tiles and, because this is a Saturday (yes, I know, an odd day to start work on a roof, but please bear with me), they will notice crowds gathering with increasing frequency at the side of the house and disappearing into the garage next to No 1 rue de Loudenne. They will hear music and laughter and will smell food. Delicious food. They will resist—but not for long, and soon they'll find themselves inside the garage, or the No 1 Saturday Market as it will be called. They'll walk past stalls packed with glorious vegetables, cheeses, and fruit; oyster stands bustling with talk and wine; old men selling eggs and onions; rows of breads—and finally arrive at a simply but beautifully decorated stall selling tempting but reasonably priced seasonal snacks. Before they have time to order, a young man will present himself and tell them that arrangements have already been made for their lunch. He will lead them through the garage, into the (by then) restored wine cellar, between rows of the finest Médoc wines, through a pantry filled with flowers and jars of jam and pork, through a little door into a large kitchen with red and white tiles and a grand fireplace. There will be duck breasts slowly grilling on dried grapevine branches, and a young woman will be giving a group of people from Bordeaux a wine-tasting class at the old kitchen table, the one that has always been in this house. "That's my cousin," the young man will say. "She's a character." He will lead the artisans through the second kitchen, through the green dining room, the one with the painting of the sly fox. Then they will arrive in the harvest room where a huge table will be beautifully laid out for twenty people, filled with flowers and candles and stacks of seasonal fruits. Everybody will have Champagne and radishes, with salt and thick yellow butter.

Puppies will be playing under the table and little children will be running around it. Soon a handsome man in his fifties will appear from the "*boucherie*" holding a big bowl of gazpacho. "That's my father," the young man will say. "He is a fabulous cook; he grew up in the kitchen and knows my great-grandmother's recipes better than anyone." Then they will have grilled meat and garlic potatoes and drink great wine served by the young woman. The lunch will last for hours, and at the end of it, the young man will tell the artisans to take the day off. "But don't tell my great-aunt Louise. She's not here today, but she's kind of strict." Then the artisans will head home, well fed and happy, ready to commence the work in earnest on Monday.

Some weeks later, a group of people, many of them family, will be gazing up at the newly tiled roof from amongst the olive trees in the garden. They will admire the work silently until one of them says, "I bet this will last for a hundred years."

ACKNOWLEDGMENTS

Thank you to:

Oddur, for everything. We are two heads on the same dragon. I love you.

Gunnhildur, Þórir, Mia, Hudson, Louise, Gaïa, and Audrey, for making my life beautiful, for your willingness to eat everything, and for (mostly) keeping your elbows off the table.

Rica, my dear editor and friend, I can´t imagine ever working on any book without your insights, efficiency, humor, and kindness.

Cyrille, for lending me your gorgeous scallops recipe and also your gentle hand in the restaurant when a real pro was needed.

Matt and Yolanda, for being such good friends and future neighbors and so supportive in everything I do—St Yzans style.

Fabien and Flo, for your endless generosity and friendship.

The dream team at Clarkson Potter, especially Anna and Kevin, my partners in crime on the publicity and marketing circuit.

Jenny, for designing such a gorgeous book, and Stephanie, Luisa, Kim, and Patricia, for taking care of it along the way.

April and Miles, for the fun we had before, during, and after meals.

Bruno Borie, for the good times in the kitchen and for all your wine we enjoyed together.

Laurent Dufau and Sophie Marc, for your support, the meals, and especially the wine we had.

Jean-Claude Ladra, for helping us understand 1 rue de Loudenne and St Yzans.

Monsieur Teyssier, for letting us use your land to grow vegetables and let our dogs run free.

Anne and Mimi, for your elegance, kindness, and all the wonderful objects that used to be in your store in St Christoly but are now in our house. And for coming to our restaurant almost every time we were open.

My parents, Genevieve and Louis, for teaching me how to love food if not to cook.

Taty Francine, for inspiring me to always make every meal special.

Jóhanna and Þórir, for your unlimited kindness, patience, and support.

Allegra, for being by my side in the kitchen every day and for being so wonderful.

Jean-Michel Cazes and your wonderful family, for lending us the keys to Médoc. So many things would not have been possible without you. And thank you for caring so much about our region.

. . . and, finally, the black cat in the village. I know who you are!

INDEX

Note: Page references in *italics* indicate photographs.

Readers everywhere fell in love with Mimi Thorisson, her family, and their band of smooth fox terriers through her blog, *Manger*, and debut cookbook, *A Kitchen in France*. In *French Country Cooking*, the family moves to an abandoned old château in Médoc. While shopping for local ingredients, cooking, and renovating the house, Mimi meets the farmers and artisans who populate the village and learns about the former owner of the house, an accomplished local cook. Here are recipes inspired by this eccentric cast of characters, including White Asparagus Soufflé, Wine Harvest Pot-au-Feu, Endives with Ham, and Salted Butter Chocolate Cake. Featuring evocative photographs taken by Mimi's husband, Oddur, this cookbook is a charming jaunt to an untouched corner of France that has thus far eluded the spotlight.

MIMI THORISSON is the author of *A Kitchen in France* and *Manger,* a blog devoted to French cooking and her life in the French countryside. She is the host of the French cooking shows *La Table de Mimi* and *Les Desserts de Mimi.* She lives with her husband, their children, and their smooth fox terriers in St Yzans, in the Médoc region of France.

Also available as an ebook

COVER DESIGN: JENNIFER K. BEAL DAVIS AND STEPHANIE HUNTWORK
COVER PHOTOGRAPHS: ODDUR THORISSON

CLARKSON POTTER/PUBLISHERS
New York
crownpublishing.com | clarksonpotter.com

La cimetière

Le chai

Le potager